MODELLING HISTORIC RAILWAYS

MODELLING HISTORIC RAILWAYS

DAVID JENKINSON

 Patrick Stephens, Wellingborough

First published in 1985

Title page Limited space need not mean the loss
of realism and this picture of 'Garsdale Road'
shows how something of the linearity of the prototype can be achieved. The gentle curve from this
viewpoint contributes more to the apparent length
than a straight run of track would have done. In
one of the more subtle tricks used to suggest
period the Class '4' 0–6–0 in the foreground was
left almost as built and given a livery introduced
around 1937, while the 0–8–0 approaching the
camera was given an earlier style and quite heavily
weathered (*Brian Monaghan*).

British Library Cataloguing in Publication Data

Jenkinson, David
   Modelling historic railways
   1. Railroads—Models
   I. Title
   625.1'9   TF197

   ISBN 0-85059-731-5

*Patrick Stephens Limited is part of the
Thorsons Publishing Group.*

Photoset in 10pt Plantin by J & L Composition
Limited, Filey, North Yorks.
Printed in Great Britain on 115 gsm Fineblade
coated cartridge, and bound, by
The Garden City Press, Letchworth, Herts,
for the publishers, Patrick Stephens Limited
Denington Estate, Wellingborough, Northants,
NN8 2QD, England

Contents

Plate 14 Dent station was and, at the time of writing, still is the highest main line station in England at which passenger trains occasionally stop. I have used this fine recent view to demonstrate how much of the character of the railway was visible until very recently. The signals and foreground sidings have now vanished but the structures are still there. If one disregards the fenced off platform building and the all too obvious signs of preserved main line steam enthusiasm, it is not very different from earlier days. The locomotive is, of course, the preserved 'Jubilee' No 5690 *Leander* — perhaps as typical as any currently to be seen on this route — and the date was July 3 1980 (*John S. Whiteley*).

14

Foreword

When I first started making railway models way back in my teens, the thought that one day I would be asked to write a book about my activities would have been inconceivable. I was brought up at the feet of such giants of model railway literature as Edward Beal, John Ahern, J. N. Maskelyne, Peter Denny and many others and I was content to read their books and articles and try to emulate their example.

My own writing started by accident. During the early 1950s, I surveyed a few prototype stations and sent off the details to one of the model magazines more in hope than expectation — and they were published. And then came what I now realise was the real beginning when, after many years of messing about, I began to follow a more consistent course of action.

I wrote a few articles about my early models and found I rather liked the business of putting pen to paper. It also seemed to strike a sympathetic chord amongst readers and the output increased, including books as well, until the point was reached when I realised that the pen was a far more powerful instrument than I had ever thought possible. It had honestly never occurred to me that so many people would be sufficiently interested in what I had to say to take up their pens and write to me, usually in friendly tones.

So much has this hobby taken hold of my spare time, largely through my writing, that I find it difficult to think of that phase when my friends were not mostly to be found amongst the ranks of railway devotees.

If, therefore, this book is of interest and the information in it is of value, the credit is due as much to my friends, whose ideas I have evaluated, whose knowledge I have unashamedly plucked and whose encouragement has kept me going, as it is to me. So it is with a real sense of gratitude that I dedicate this book:

To my friends in the hobby — with my sincere thanks.

David Jenkinson
Knaresborough, January 1985

Chapter 1

The search for a modelling philosophy

'Railway modelling is a pleasure rather than a fad and should be free from the pedantry which dictates. Yet our aim in this writing is to indicate a consistent course of action . . .'

E. Beal, *Modelling the Old-Time Railways*

I would think that many modellers in the miniature scales who grew up in this hobby either just before or just after the Second World War were strongly influenced by the phenomenal writing and modelling output of that doyen of our craft, Edward Beal; and although I cannot, in truth, claim to have been influenced by all of his ideas, I still regard the quotation at the head of this page as possibly the most significant 32 words ever written on the subject. Yet it was probably ten years or more after I seriously started making my own model railways before I read the book from which it is taken. Since then I have used the quotation many times and if I have a modelling philosophy at all, it is, I hope, essentially summed up by Edward Beal's final words — 'a consistent course of action'.

In my writing on the subject of railway modelling I have always tried to help modellers, especially beginners, from falling into traps and finding themselves heading up blind alleys. I have done this for the most part in the hope that by discussing some of the principles which appear to me to make sense, others might thereby be helped to save themselves the time and trouble of finding out the hard way — as I did. Little of what I have done is earth shatteringly original but a brief digression as to how and why I have arrived at my present attitudes may prove of interest in establishing the theme of this book.

The growth of interest

I have often been asked why I am interested in railways and why I make models of them.

To neither question can I give a wholly satisfactory answer — nor, in retrospect, do I think it matters over much. As a small child I was taken to 'meet Daddy's train from the office' and my dear old Mum, never realising what she had started, always used to arrive at the station well in advance of my father's train. We had moved to South London from Yorkshire at the time and all I can remember, and that vaguely, is the all-pervading green of the old Southern Railway and the infinite superiority (to my young mind) of the steam-hauled expresses, which never deigned to stop, compared with the humdrum electrics which were the only sort of trains I ever got to ride on.

My only travels on 'real' trains (as I had now begun to regard the locomotive-hauled versions) were on the somewhat infrequent trips north for family reunions at summer and Christmas time. It is small wonder, what with the prospect of indulgent relatives at the far end coupled with the promise of riding on a proper train, that I began to regard the railways at St Pancras and Kings Cross with infinitely more regard than I ever did their opposite numbers at Waterloo and Charing Cross. And I had never heard of Paddington!

I'm not sure which route to Leeds we used most often — the Midland or the GN — although I can clearly recall, with some terror, being lifted by a kind engine driver onto the footplate of a huge silver-grey monster at Kings Cross station after a southbound journey. It must have been one of the 'Silver' series of 'A4's but what it was doing on the Leeds–Kings Cross service in 1936/7 I do not know. However, the most vivid memory is of my first northbound trip from St Pancras. Father had chosen the Midland route because 'It is not so crowded and the LMS coaches are more comfortable' but the ritual of 'looking at the engine' still had to be carried out. My first surprise was that the train was a red one — I'd never seen a red train before — but this was as nothing compared with my first view of a red engine, beautifully clean, glinting in the sunshine. I have never got over that feeling — although I cannot remember what the engine was (probably a 'Jubilee' or a Compound); and my developing brain instantly concluded that any railway which could paint its engines this fabulous colour simply had to be the most superior system in the land!

I know now that I was probably lucky to see a clean red engine on the LMS in the late 1930s and that the company was not entirely perfect but I can honestly say that my real

Plates 1 and 2 *Scenes from Childhood* It is likely that most modellers come into the hobby as a result of vividly remembered scenes from their youth and these two pictures serve to remind me of the initial 'triggers' to my own interest. I include them here, partly because they are nice pictures but also because they demonstrate, to me, how much more use a picture can be if one is prepared to do a little research — see Chapter 5.

The upper view is of a Southern Railway train, sometime in the 1930s at a location which I cannot identify. Trains like this were once a familiar sight to me. The second picture can tell me much more. It shows LMS Class '5XP' 4–6–0 No 5570 *New Zealand* leaving St Pancras on a northbound express and I can date the picture no earlier than c 1937–38 — the engine has received a domed boiler and is carrying the red shaded yellow insignia which the LMS did not introduce until 1937. The leading carriage is one of a series of flush sided 'square windowed' open thirds built just prior to Stanier's arrival, during 1931–2 and is carrying the fully lined livery, abandoned in 1934. Now the LMS painted its carriages every seven years or so, as a general rule, so this carriage is probably less than seven years old — or it would be in the simple livery of the second vehicle in the train. It seems too clean, as does the engine, for them both to be post-war survivors in pre-war colours so I reckon 1938 or 1939 is a good bet (*NRM, BR LMR*).

interest in railways in general and the LMS in particular was probably stimulated more by this vivid experience as a small boy than almost anything which has happened since. And I still get the same thrill whenever I see a clean red engine with steam in her belly and fire in her heart. Stupid really ... but I digress.

Railway models entered the proceedings at about the same time. Naturally, young Jenkinson wanted a red engine and it duly emerged as a clockwork Gauge '0' Hornby Compound *No 1185*, followed about a year later by a Bassett-Lowke *Princess Elizabeth*. Father had, meantime, scratchbuilt a Gauge '0' Jubilee (still, happily, in existence) and we ran the trains on elevated track in the garden — no scenery or anything like that but it was fun.

Came the war and a move back to Yorkshire; and the garden railway was re-erected at the new house. Supplies were difficult and the stock situation never progressed much beyond that which existed in 1939, but for six more years we ran trains in the garden on a simple layout whose track plan is still etched in my mind. We also had some tinplate track for indoor work but the outdoor railway utilised handbuilt track and I suppose that struck something of a chord too. At all events, when the war was over and I decided to build my own railway models, it never even occurred to me that one could actually buy ready made track — and I never did, until much later and for totally different reasons.

During the next 10 to 15 years when money (or the lack of it) was the over-riding consideration, I built two '00' layouts (neither of them finished), dabbled with kits, tackled a bit of rudimentary scratch building but generally did nothing of great note at all. In spite of wide reading, my activities lacked direction and purpose and an inventory of my models in 1961 revealed three pre-BR British companies, two American ones, a set of Kitmaster 'Blue' Pullmans and a train of BR Mk I stock. The only common factor was track gauge and all told it was not the most exhilarating collection on which to build an empire. It was about this time that Edward Beal came to the rescue with his 'consistent course of action' — and I sold off everything, save for a few reasonably respectable LMS carriages.

Now I mention all these early activities, not because they are of any great significance

in themselves, but in order to show just what sort of a 'dog's breakfast' can result from a prolonged period of aimless modelling. I can well understand why many people give up altogether and I suppose it was only my deep-seated love for all railways that kept me in the hobby. Looking back on this period, I am convinced that the major lesson to be learned was the importance of deciding at the outset exactly what is required and pursuing this aim fairly relentlessly, refusing to be diverted into interesting by-ways. Paradoxically, more genuine enjoyment seems to result.

Not that the early period was entirely wasted — far from it. I acquired, from necessity, quite an amount of scratch building experience. I experienced the joys (and sorrows) of trying to make my first white metal kit hold together or get my first handbuilt track to work. Most important of all, when I finally rationalised the situation, it did help me to decide what I wanted and above all what I did not want from future models. Thus, I would conclude that it is no bad thing for a modeller to go through an 'indecisive' period — but I would not recommend he allows it to last for 15 years! It is foolish to believe that one's first model(s) will last a lifetime but I am convinced that consistency of approach is the most likely to pay dividends in the long run.

Having, therefore, thought out all these matters, I decided to have a fresh start and I have been trying during the last 20 years or so to create models based on what I pompously call 'fine scale principles based on a consistent course of action'. If I have achieved any measure of success, it is probably more by virtue of being a good cribber rather than any special model-making skill. Therefore, I do not propose to burden readers with my solutions to the problems of making intransigent objects adhere to impossible surfaces — there are others far more fitted to do so — but I would like to discuss some of the *ideas* which I think are important if one wants to build a model railway.

We live in an age of specialists and I mean no disrespect to these gentlemen when I say that, for me, there is no intrinsic interest in modelling a series of company gas lamps or signal finials. My goal is a model railway in every sense of the word and since we are on this earth for only a limited life-span and my pocket is not bottomless, I cannot afford the time (or its most usual substitute — money) to devote two years to one engine or a lifetime

Plates 3 and 4 *Enter the Settle-Carlisle* To most people, Ribblehead signifies the Settle and Carlisle railway and I can truthfully say that my first awareness of the railway was gained in this very spot. The wide open spaces, almost barren of vegetation, Class '4' 0–6–0 goods engines plodding away on almost every type of train and always a suggestion that the weather might turn fickle are my earliest memories of this place and it has not changed much.

In modelling terms, this sort of scene is really too vast to create but it holds a few clues which can help. Note, for example the embankment ahead of the engines on both pictures. On the picture showing the full length of the viaduct, the view is of the north side and it is still almost as rock strewn as when the navvies built it some 80 years earlier — even the grass is having a hard time of it. The embankment in front of the engineers' train faces south (roughly) and here a few stunted trees have managed to take hold — but not very many. Attention to detail like this can suggest the nature of the countryside even if space is limited in the model (*W. Hubert Foster — courtesy NRM; Eric Treacy — courtesy P. B. Whitehouse*).

to station footbridge design. However, I do have a great love of railways and to this end the finished product has to look as nearly right as possible. A super detailed engine against a hastily knocked up background is far worse to me than a well-assembled kit in a proper setting and I would rather have a loco 2 mm out in wheelbase if (but only 'if') the price of 100 per cent accuracy is no time to build a layout to run it on.

My overall aim is to try and reflect in miniature those features of railways which most appeal to me. To this end, I am neither for or against the 100 per cent super-detail approach but am trying something which I feel is more important. I would like to think of our hobby as presenting something more than the conventional image of grown men playing trains. I, for one, can see no reason why railway modelling should not aspire to some, at least, of the status accorded to other creative activities — music, art, etc; yet I sometimes wonder if some modellers have any feeling at all for the objects they are trying to portray. Perhaps I am chasing moonbeams — I do not know. All I do know is that while there are plenty of books and articles on how to make this or that, there are precious few on why we do it. Perhaps it does not matter to many people but it fascinates me and I am using my own chosen prototype in this book, not with the idea of making converts, far from it, but merely for the purpose of illustrating principles which are, perhaps, often overlooked in our strivings after rivet detail.

Concerning the prototype itself, it is impossible to know too much if one is trying to create atmosphere in a model. Especially must we pay attention to those aspects which distinguish one piece of railway from another. It is impossible in a word to say what it is that, even in 1985, still makes certain stretches of railway obviously 'Midland' or 'Great Northern' or what have you, so I will merely attempt it for one piece of railway and leave it to others to do the same for their own favourites.

The real beginning

Imagine yourself, one cool morning in early spring some 20 or 30 years ago standing on the south-east flank of Blea Moor, looking north over the roof of Yorkshire. There is probably still snow about and a howling gale, or at least a stiff breeze, is causing you to pull your coat tighter. Apart from a few half-frozen sheep, there is not a soul in sight, probably not even a house. Other than the wind, you are alone with thoughts until you hear the sound of a train behind your shoulder. Turn round and what do you see? It could be an express speeding south at 70 plus but more likely it is a goods engine hammering its way ponderously over a gigantic viaduct as it reaches the last of 14 miles of almost continuous 1 in 100 grade to Blea Moor Tunnel with 30 or more heavily loaded wagons in tow. This is no sleepy rural branch line, though the scene is pastoral enough, but a real main line with long trains and clearly built to last. What is it doing here? Why, in the middle of nowhere, do we find these enormous earthworks and engineering features? Who built it and why choose this desolate spot? These were the questions I asked myself and I knew I had to find the answer. To those similarly afflicted, the symptoms of the disease are known well enough and, fortunately, there is no known cure!

I think I can say with some justification, albeit tinged with a little prejudice, that this famous line, the Settle and Carlisle, is as magnificent a piece of railway as any in Britain; certainly, in my view, only the West Highland can compete and that is single track. Nothing comparable ever emanated from Paddington or Waterloo! Born out of a spirit of Victorian competition, it was built in the early 1870s at a time when much was known of the art of railway building. As a result, it is superbly engineered and because it was conceived as an entity, has none of the piecemeal look of so many British lines which are an amalgam of several companies' routes. The Midland wanted to get to Scotland and, being the Midland, there were to be no half measures about it. No poky little wooden huts apologising as stations, no primitive lean-to sheds masquerading as goods depots and when it came to obstacles, of which there were one or two, these seemed to present an inspiration rather than a problem. Thus, the final product stands as a 110 year-old tribute to our 19th century railway builders — the oft-derided Victorians. I wonder if anyone will be as enthusiastic about the M1 in 2069?

Then there were the trains. What could be more splendid than a Midland express in full cry? That glorious Derby red on both engine and coaches, to many the most beautiful livery of them all. My regret is that I never

5

Plate 5 I had not long been investigating the details of the Settle-Carlisle before I became aware of the superb detail of the engineering work and realised that I would have to photograph much of it myself. I naturally had a go at all the big structures but, in modelling terms, the smaller features were just as well engineered. Look, for example at the superb masonry detail in this eminently modellable three-arch bridge in the Ribble gorge between Stainforth and Helwith Bridge. It would not be necessary to know the precise dimensions of a structure such as this to capture its essential nature (*D. Jenkinson*).

knew it personally, but can only look at pictures or museum exhibits. The LMS very sensibly perpetuated this scheme, not perhaps as successfully, but, at least the thought was there. Yes, there was more than some justification for the Midland's slogan: 'The Best Route' and those of us who follow LMS practice can be thankful that this fine company inherited the Midland's ways — too much so according to some followers of the Euston regime!

What, then, is this Settle and Carlisle like, which has caused so much to be written and which, for an inanimate object, has an uncanny way of insinuating itself into the minds of those who know it? I do not know that I can answer all of this but I will have a try. I have analysed the line fully in another book,* so here I will concentrate on those 'atmospheric' aspects which have been the inspiration of my modelling activities.

To savour to the full its fascination, we have to go back to the very foundations of the Midland Railway Company. Many will know

* *Rails in the Fells*, Peco Publications 1973, 1980.

that the first ever route from London to Scotland went via Rugby and York, between which two places it ran over the metals of what became the central portion of the Midland Railway. This early association with the Scottish traffic, coupled with the piratical antics of the LNWR and the unmentionable upstarts from Kings Cross (both of whom managed to dispense with the Midland, reaching Scotland via the West and East coast routes respectively) left behind in the Midland boardroom an obsessional complex about Scottish traffic. The Midland directors gradually extended their empire further and further from Derby until they found themselves (by dint of having collared from under Euston's nose the 'Little' North Western from Skipton to Ingleton) with an outlet to Scotland via Tebay. The only trouble was that, in order to take advantage of it, they had to hand over their traffic at this latter point to the LNWR!

Now the LNWR was wont to treat the Midland's traffic in very cavalier fashion. This, to put it mildly, was not well received at Derby and much discussion must have

6

Plate 6 Dent Head and Dentdale represent another part of the route which captures the imagination — this is the classic view from the road entering from the top of the valley. The back lighting helps draw attention to the projecting rows of masonry just below the arches of the viaduct — put there initially to support the wooden formers used when building the structure. Dry stone walls, sparse vegetation and few signs of human habitation all add to the impression of a wide open wilderness (*D. Jenkinson collection*).

Plate 7 Settle and Carlisle stations were built to last — this is Kirkby Stephen in 1962, the train being a southbound fitted freight headed by one of the ubiquitous Class '5' 4–6–0s, No 44943. Note how much peripheral detail can be taken from this picture — the neatly coursed masonry of the station and walls, the much larger random stone supports for the platform, the original Midland bargeboards on the gable ends and, in the left background, a Midland platform-end water column (*D. Jenkinson*).

7

Plates 8 and 9 These two pictures represent between them the best part of half a century of express travel on the Leeds-Carlisle line. Plate 8 shows a double-headed train in the mid-1920s, hardly changed in colour, carriage type or motive power since the Midland Railway of Edwardian days. Only the LMS crests, faintly visible on the cab sides and the elliptical roof carriages of the first LMS series of coaching stock reveal the post-grouping influence. Even the second vehicle (ex-West Coast joint stock) might have been seen in earlier days as a through portion.

The second view, taken at a classic Settle-Carlisle location, Ais Gill, in 1948, shows the final LMS type of train and locomotive which did not become seriously 'diluted' by BR influence, save in terms of livery changes, until well into the 1950s. The locomotive and carriages are both of the Stanier breed, save for the slightly earlier 12 wheel dining car in the middle of the train. The engine is Leeds based 'Jubilee' No 45611 *Hong Kong* (*W. Hubert Foster — courtesy NRM*).

taken place there. Be that as it may, in 1865, the Derby men decided, as they had in the case of their entry to London via Hitchin and the GNR, that the only solution was to cock a snook at the opposition and build their own route to Scotland from Settle via the 'Little' North Western.

The Euston directors were not unduly perturbed at this idea — why should they be? They had seen the area involved, already pronounced uncrossable by more than one engineer, and if the Midland wanted to bankrupt itself in going over the Pennines in order to get to Carlisle, it was OK by them. However, the Midland's bill passed Parliament in 1866 and it seemed that the Derby folk were intent on business — or were they? The Derby motives are a little vague here, but they must have worked. At all events, it seems the LNWR got cold feet for a time (perhaps prompted by some of the Midland shareholders!) and made a very fair offer of sharing running powers over the West coast line north of Tebay. The Midland, delighted

at having got what it wanted, promptly proposed to abandon the folly in the mountains; but Derby had underestimated the opposition! Furious protests rolled in from, amongst others, the L&YR and NBR, not to mention the local gentry who wanted a new railway. The abandonment bill was thrown out! The Midland, now completely hoist with its own petard, gave a sickly grin and decided it had better start building — and thus, as much by accident as by design, the 'Long Drag' was under way.

Work started in 1869 but the first passenger trains did not run until 1876. At times the company must have wondered if it would ever be finished. Both cost and time taken were 50 per cent over estimate, at least one contractor went bankrupt and over 100 workmen died in the mountains around Blea Moor alone. Who, looking from the train as it crosses Ribblehead viaduct, can imagine that here was a shanty town of over 2,000 people? Now there is nothing. In the 1870s, the fells rang with the shouts of bare knuckle

Plate 10 This timeless view shows the waste land of Batty Moss with a southbound express hurrying south in front of a cloud-topped Ingleborough. It is hard to believe that the whole of the barren foreground area was once a shanty town of over 2,000 people during the building of the railway. Only the rather large number of motor cars parked along the roadside reveal that this picture is not all that it seems. The engine is the preserved *Duchess of Hamilton* and the date was February 11 1984! Note how insignificant both the 13 coach train and Ribblehead station seem in this wild landscape (*Barry Lane*).

10

Plates 11 and 12 These two 'train-less' pictures have been included to show the magnificent 'high-speed' alignment of the Settle-Carlisle as it traverses the Pennine watershed at over 1,100 ft above sea level. The first view, looking in a southerly direction from Dent station shows the bare hillsides and snow fences to perfection and was taken in 1946 as also was the second view, looking north over the celebrated water troughs near Garsdale. The station itself is just beyond the overbridge in the distance, beyond which the line swings left in front of the far range of hills as it heads for Ais Gill Summit. Both scenes are magnificent and equally unmodellable! (*W. Hubert Foster — courtesy NRM*).

fights to find the 'cock' of the camp and the company even felt obliged to provide missionaries for the spiritual needs of these wild men of the moors.

Only the ghosts of these men remain with a 72-mile monument which, itself their finest memorial, proves that for all the fights and ale swilling, these men knew their job. Blea Moor and Rise Hill tunnels were hewn out of solid rock, Ribblehead viaduct is $\frac{1}{4}$ mile long, 105 ft high and contains single blocks of stone weighing up to eight tons each. Nor

were these and others like them the only feats. Nature herself had posed a few problems of no mean order. Embankments refused to bind, whole hillsides began to slide bodily into the valleys and at Dandry Mire, for two years, the peat swallowed up all the tipped material which should have been rising as an embankment, so much so that they built a ten-arch viaduct instead! The Midland had no choice; it could go round, go through, go over or go under the obstacles; but go it must and go it did.

Plate 13 '. . . the sort of weather to which perhaps only Wagner could have done justice'. I always feel that when the Settle and Carlisle is in this sort of mood it is at its most dramatic. You cannot model it but you can still experience the feeling, if you are lucky; for this view too is modern — *Duchess of Hamilton* again, only a few seconds before Plate 10 was taken (*Barry Lane*).

The problems were not made any easier by the fact that this line was to be a main line, fully competitive with the East and West coast routes, with a ruling gradient of 1 in 100 and no sharp bends. They got their ruling gradient (plenty of it — ask any fireman!) and they got their alignment but at a prodigious cost in materials and man power. Small wonder that the retiring general manager of the Midland, Mr James Allport, wanted Blea Moor painted in the background of his official portrait — the company was almost buried there! No, this railway does not wind through the hills and the trains do not crawl along the valleys. Poised over 1,100 ft above sea-level, the trains sweep past the heads of the valleys and the one-time scenes of hectic activity at some 70 mph plus while the uninitiated passenger, may he be forgiven for it, either sleeps or eats his lunch! No, the early engineers built well and until recent years there was not one speed restriction below the overall limit for the line.

To appreciate all this at its grandest you have to have the right sort of weather — storm clouds, howling winds and driving rain — the sort of weather to which perhaps only Wagner could have done justice. The weather is never far from the surface up here and stories of its antics are legion, like that of

the fireman whose cap was blown off on Ribblehead viaduct, swept through the arches and then, in a sort of eddy, supposedly blown back on to the engine again! Then there was the train which waited for over five minutes at Ribblehead station before the doors could be opened in a gale. Other stories are more substantially founded, however. Many a farmer has mysteriously 'acquired' a new haystack cover (blown off a passing goods truck!) and trains have often been beaten to a standstill on Ribblehead viaduct by the wind. As recently as 1964/5, a consignment of cars was unceremoniously removed from a train. There are huge fences along the lineside near Dent to hold back the snow — much good these were in winters like '47 or '63 — but the best weather story of all is probably that of the Garsdale turntable, now, alas, removed for ever.

At first sight it may seem odd that there was a turntable here at all since it was at the opposite side of the line from its most likely customers, engines off the Hawes branch, but in the old MR days, Garsdale throbbed with activity. The Midland's was a 'little and often' policy in regard to motive power and therefore on this line, most loads of any size had to be piloted. It being more convenient to pilot in both directions than to use

Plate 14 appears on page 6.

Plate 15 The famous stockaded turntable at Garsdale was another Settle-Carlisle legend — and could at least be modelled if one was so-minded — but it was fortunate indeed if one actually caught an engine using it after the closure of the Hawes branch. As far as I know, only the daily pick-up freight engine took advantage during later steam days — and then not always. I was lucky enough to find it in use in May 1963 and, although the weather was its usual perverse self, managed to get this picture. I never saw it used again (*D. Jenkinson*).

15

Plate 16 The sylvan scenery of the Eden gorge near Baron Wood was never photographed very much in earlier days but this fine modern picture gives a very good idea of the contrast from the high fells to the south. I include this picture for purely selfish reasons. The date was April 26 1980 and I had been asked at short notice by the then owners to help service and turn *Leander* at Carlisle. Much to my joy I was offered a footplate ride back to Appleby as a reward for an hour of coal heaving and I just happened to stick my head out of the cab when this picture was taken — moreover we came up the hill to Appleby in less than the booked time for a Class '47' diesel! (*John S. Whiteley*).

16

bankers, Garsdale grew as the place where the pilots were turned before sending them back down again. One night, they were turning a loco at Garsdale when it was caught broadside on by a severe wind. Now there is little to stop an east wind between here and Central Europe so the engine went on spinning for hours like a merry-go-round. It was only stopped by pouring sand into the well of the turntable. The story does not say how the sand was moved out again, but the turntable was later surrounded by a sleeper-built stockade, which feature it retained to the end, to prevent any repetition of that particular incident.

However, the Settle and Carlisle has another side. From the wild mountains it drops to the lovely Eden valley and in following this river from Appleby to Carlisle there is no hint of the rugged country behind. Green fields, wooded slopes, the Lake District mountains in the far West and the giant scarp of the Pennines close by on the East, give an almost magical quality to the scene. As the valley broadens and the line reaches its destination, it seems somehow fitting that it should attain its goal in so peaceful a fashion.

So much for the line itself, but in its heyday the Settle and Carlisle was not just a railway but an institution. It was the very lifeline of the remote communities in the area who regarded it, as should be the case, as a worthy friend. Even writers who had no background of railway enthusiasm noticed

Plates 17 and 18 An essential part of the Settle and Carlisle scene is represented by the various clusters of 'domestic' buildings located along the route. Two typical examples are shown here, both photographed in 1963, as I recall. The stepped terrace at Garsdale (Plate 17), with its semi-rustic front porches, is highly characteristic — and those porches are no cosmetic decoration in bad weather either! The other view shows the lonely 'settlement' at Blea Moor, just north of the signal box. It features an alternative type of stone cottage along with a somewhat more modern house (*D. Jenkinson*).

this fact and commented on how little, if any, the line jarred the scene. Of course, to a bigot like myself, it positively enhances it, but unless you have been there you cannot know this sensation. What is even more noticeable is the way in which the line affects the scene outside the boundary fences. Virtually every house at Garsdale Head was built by the railway — they had to be since there was no settlement here before. Not only that, but the water tank house served as the local village hall on more than one occasion. Lonely cottages at Blea Moor and Aisgill stand guard over the railway and once housed the men who saw the trains safely through. The stationmaster at Dent (only five miles from the village) lived in a house with double glazed windows (built in the 1870s!) while as many know, Ribblehead station had a harmonium in the waiting-room for occasional church services. This line 'belonged' to its setting and its folk. The prospect of possible closure is, to say the least, heartbreaking (written in 1984 at the time of the closure threat).

Strange thoughts these, you may say, in a work devoted to the art of Railway Modelling, but if I have managed to give you some idea of the 'flavour' of the line, it may make sense when I say that somewhere in all this lay the reason why I had to try to model it and I can only say to those who do not look at things in quite this way, that I think they are missing a very great deal. To me, this sort of approach is an essential ingredient for a model railway, even though I have no wish to sound dogmatic. It was my good fortune that the Settle and Carlisle happened to belong to the particular company which had fired my imagination as a small boy — the LMS — so it was not too difficult to marry my two main interests and I have never regretted the decision. I have, however, often wondered what I might have done had the Settle and Carlisle belonged to the LNER!

Anyway, for 20 years or more I have been trying to model this fascinating railway and the enthusiasm has never really waned. I have completed three EM Gauge 4 mm scale layouts based on the theme and developed

Plate 19 While it is impossible to put back the clock and return to former days, the enthusiasm of the BR locomen has become legendary during the last few years as they have re-familiarised themselves with steam power on this route. Of course, the engines these days are cleaner and probably better maintained than in the final steam years and you cannot escape the flotilla of motor cars; but when a scene like this greets your eyes, it is hard to remain unmoved. This is *Duchess of Hamilton* yet again, northbound on the 'Long Drag' near Stainforth on February 4 1984 climbing the 1 in 100 at about 50 mph with a 450-ton train. If nothing else, it symbolises the 'man against the elements' theme which really sums-up the Settle-Carlisle railway. One wonders whether it can possibly last much longer (*Barry Lane*).

19

Plates 20 and 21 These two pictures show the first two attempts in 4 mm scale to re-create something of the Settle-Carlisle 'feel' in model form. The view of 'Marthwaite' shows it as originally built in 1963. The buildings were all modelled from the prototype but my knowledge was a bit 'thin' at that time so I do not think it really caught the remoteness of the region. The yard looks too cramped and the lack of attention to detail makes me cringe when I look back across 20 years or more; but it was a start.

'Garsdale Road' was based on Dent and this view, taken in 1970, represents the modelled version of the real scene shown at Plate 14. By now, more attention was being paid to detail and to train formations and carriage types. I was particularly pleased with the disguised baseboard join, running left to right between engine and tender on this picture, and the track had improved a great deal. It was, however, still a little cramped and the curve through the platforms too sharp (*Jim Russell, Roy Anderson*).

my first 7 mm scale system to an operational stage before a house move forced yet another radical re-design. This proliferation may well seem at odds with my 'consistency' theme; but each and every one had its own logic within my circumstances at the time and whenever I was forced to make a fresh start, I hope I had learned a few more lessons. At all events, I am now working on a second Gauge '0' system which I think should keep me happy for years. In spite of many changes of house (six during the period 1964–71, not to mention two more since), and several excursions into other modelling fields, I always seem to come back to my primary choice — and it is the 'I' which is important. A model must, first and foremost, satisfy the wishes of its owner and creator. While it does this without serious reservation, then there is no need to succumb to the blandishments of others who will try to persuade you to change scale, standards or anything else that happens to be currently fashionable. The only time to make changes is when you, as the person most concerned, feel it to be worthwhile.

It is with this background in mind that I have prepared this book. It is not a treatise for the engineer, nor a series of 'how to do it' instructions about the actual business of model building. What I have tried to do is analyse the problems and difficulties involved when trying to model the historical prototype — in my case the Settle and Carlisle — in the hope that others may thereby be helped. Although I shall use the Settle and Carlisle for most of the examples I quote, I am not trying to make converts to my own choice of prototype — although that would be nice — but I would be flattered if I made a few converts to my own way of thinking about the problems involved in tackling what I like to call the 'total railway' approach.

I am principally interested in the model railway as a *totality* and all my ideas have been evolved against a wish to build a complete model railway in every sense of the word. If this is in the reader's mind too, then my hope is that he or she will find something of interest within these pages, regardless of chosen prototype.

I have deliberately omitted a map of the Settle and Carlisle line since it did not seem entirely relevant to the theme of the book. However, for modelmakers, a much more useful document is the so-called 'sidestrip' diagram which the LMS issued for almost all of its lines. I have, therefore, reproduced the full Settle and Carlisle version in Appendix IV. It well repays careful study, whether or not this particular route is your chosen prototype.

Chapter 2

The need for discrimination

'The art of discrimination is not to let the other chap do all the discriminating for you!'

Anonymous

The only single theme which binds this work together is my assumption that the reader wishes to model some sort of 'historic' railway scene. But since railway history sometimes seems to begin in the mists of antiquity and ends, literally, yesterday, it follows that one has to be selective in one's choice and fairly rigorous in keeping to the 'straight and narrow' as it were. To do this involves discrimination and, in the broadest sense, this in turn resolves itself to two, apparently quite simple, considerations, the choice and nature of the prototype to be tackled and the type of model desired.

The two are, of course, closely related and in the detailed planning stages of an historical model railway they tend to become inextricably intertwined. However, in order to try and bring order out of chaos, I will at this stage deal with them separately; they will be linked later. However, before tackling even these two issues, it is, perhaps, as well to define what is meant by an 'historical' model railway, or, more specifically, in this case, how I as author, choose to define the subject – for it is necessity a personal choice, different for each of us.

I have never, in any of my writing, tried to assert that my approach to the subject is the only way to proceed, nor do I wish to do so now — but it is important for a reader to know the opinions, prejudices and attitudes of a writer in order to assess the value of the end product. So let me state from the outset, that for me, the question of historical modelling comes down to but two considerations. The first I have already mentioned at the end of Chapter 1 — the 'total' railway concept. The second is the need for 'atmosphere' in

the finished model. Funnily enough, these two are closely allied to the basic considerations mentioned in the first paragraph of this chapter. The choice of prototype is bound up with one's perception of 'railway atmosphere' and the type of model to be made seems to me to be inevitably determined by the modeller's view of what the overall end product should be. Speaking personally, however, I do think it is difficult to create 'atmosphere' except in the context of a complete model railway.

This may all seem startlingly obvious and perhaps less than wildly original but it is quite a useful starting point because it does tend to lay emphasis at the outset on the broader issues. It is important to establish the framework before filling in the details. Only when the overall theme is established to the satisfaction of the modeller is it possible to consider the detailed modelling implications.

The choice of prototype and the search for atmosphere

If it were not for that indefinable something called 'railway atmosphere' I venture to suggest there would be very few railway enthusiasts and even fewer modellers. There is something about railways, all railways, which holds an irresistible appeal to many people of whom a considerable number try to capture this 'certain something' via the modelling medium. That we don't always succeed does not stop us trying and I doubt if we often stop to analyse the sheer absurdity of it all when viewed in strictly rational terms! However, it is possible to sort things out provided we don't try too hard to explain why we do it — that is a much more complicated problem.

In the previous chapter I allowed myself a certain amount of space to try to explain something of the circumstances by which my own modelling philosophy had developed and I attempted to describe in somewhat imprecise terms the nature and character of my chosen prototype by way of demonstrating some of the issues involved. I cannot stress too strongly — or repeat too often — that this aspect of the story will differ for every one of us.

The three basic character-giving ingredients of a railway are the geographical environment, the identity (and type) of the railway within that environment and the period in time which is represented. Any 'atmosphere' the end product may display stems from these three. The relative dominance of one or another constituent in the total 'mix' can vary widely and, in choosing a prototype, the modeller may be influenced by whichever of the three ingredients is most important to him.

Starting then with the geographical location we have to remember that the landscape was there first and the railway tailored to it. Into this setting is inserted the railway and the relationships between railway and landscape are not haphazard but meaningful. The most obvious 'clues' to this relationship can be discerned from the amount and nature of the civil engineering, since the landscape itself can only provide a setting into which

the railway engineer puts his line. The response of the engineer will, largely, be determined by the economic importance of the route to be built. Thus a line likely to carry heavy and frequent traffic at high speeds will justify the use of heavy embankments, viaducts, tunnels, etc, in order to keep gradients easy and curvature gentle, whereas a small feeder line will more closely follow the natural contours at some compromise in both alignment and gradient in order to keep costs down. Thus, in a sense, one of the first decision points a modeller reaches is to determine the type and nature of line to be modelled in order that he may get the background environment properly established.

But it is not just the lie of the land which should command our attention. The character of the local architecture (particularly older buildings) often makes a region distinctive as, indeed, does the building material used. It is little use modelling a brick viaduct in what is supposed to be the heart of granite or limestone territory or putting a model of a Scottish gamekeeper's cottage in the heart of rural Wiltshire. Maybe the odd freak of this nature does occur in real life but, if so, it usually creates the sort of jarring element which we, as modellers, must take pains to avoid.

So ... study the vernacular architecture; take note of the typical disposition of buildings; analyse the distribution and type of trees; pay attention to the relative propor-

Plate 22 '... the landscape was there first ...' — and nowhere in Britain was this more obvious than on the Settle-Carlisle. A few years ago I was given a handful of old pictures of the line under construction and this one is possibly the most interesting, showing Ribblehead Viaduct under construction with the famous shanty town faintly visible in the background. The pictures at Plates 10 and 13 were taken from the crest of the rise to the extreme right of this view some 110 years later. The massive nature of the construction clearly has no explanation save in the context of the overall scheme of things. This picture reveals quite clearly that if there were need only for a local line, there was plenty of fairly flat ground at a lower level (*D. Jenkinson collection*).

22

Plates 23 and 24 These views of Crosby Garrett viaduct are separated by some 80 years or more. Plate 23 shows the structure as construction was just about finished and the cottages visible through one of the middle two arches are those in the right foreground of the second picture, taken from the opposite side c 1950. The interesting point here is not that the viaduct is Midland as such — after all, the Midland's viaducts were not all that different in style from anyone else's structures of similar type — but that the local vernacular architecture immediately gives a clue to location. That the viaduct is stone does not really help but these cottages and dry stone walls are the key. Another point to mention is the 'raw' look of the scene when the viaduct was first finished. Historical modellers setting their efforts in the middle to late Victorian period should remember that the railways were often quite new at that time and the scenery should be modelled to reflect a kind of newness. It is only with the passage of time that mature vegetation and natural weathering of the building materials impart an 'old' quality (*D. Jenkinson collection*).

Plate 25 This view at Helwith Bridge looking towards the characteristic outline of Pen-y-Ghent in the distance, reinforces the points made at Plates 23 and 24. It was taken c 1946 when the line was 70 years old; yet the road overbridge stonework still looks much newer than the rest, save where blackened (on one line only) by the smoke of uphill trains. An incidental point worth making which is clearly shown in this view is that the Settle and Carlisle boundaries are not the conventional fences but actually dry stone walls throughout most of its length. It is attention to little things like this which help establish credibility in a modelled scene (*D. Jenkinson collection*).

26

Plate 26 Occasionally, the lineside scene carries a visible reminder of its own construction which time can never remove. This view of Arten Gill Viaduct shows such a feature — the huge spoil tip seen on the hillside just behind the train with its level surface contrasting with the general left to right downwards slope of the natural hillside. The occasion was the day of the memorial service to Bishop Eric Treacy at Appleby with the preserved BR Class '9F' 2–10–0 No 92220 *Evening Star*, from the National Railway Museum, heading north on September 30 1978 (*Peter Robinson*).

Plate 27 Another detail worth noting when studying the alignment of a railway is the extent to which the original man-made features of the landscape have been modified. The example here is at Dent Head where the original local road entering the valley from the head of the dale was diverted to make way for foundation piers for the viaduct. The little bridge in the foreground carries this diverted road and was built by the Midland Railway contemporaneously with the viaduct itself (*D. Jenkinson*).

tions of arable, grass and open spaces; check on the predominant livestock type to be seen in the fields; consider the basic geological characteristics of the physical landscape . . . and so on. Then you are on the right lines to establishing 'where?' in geographical terms. At this stage if we are fortunate, we may have established a 'where' element for the potential model but the railway itself could be any company operating in such an area. The next step, therefore, is to establish what can be called a 'railway identity'.

Fortunately for British modellers, most of the popular railways had distinctive trademarks which even 60 years of grouping and nationalisation have not totally eradicated.

27

Plates 28 to 30 These three pictures have been included to show how a particular railway could place its 'trademarks' on the scene, even without there being trains present. Plate 28 shows Dent station c 1906 and amongst the typically Midland features even at this remote place can be observed platform lamps and angled nameboards, diagonal platform and conventional post and rail fencing and, in the distance, the characteristic signal box. The architecture is, of course, typical of the Midland in general but of this line in particular.

The second view, looking north at Garsdale — then called Hawes Junction — shows some of the same features along with platform barrows and seats. The Midland signals are a bit more obvious in this picture at the far end and at this time (also c 1906) the station had a platform awning protecting the 'interchange' area between the main line and branch trains. The far end of this awning is more typically Midland in style. Note the lack of human population on both this and the previous picture — people in this part of the world did not remain in the open air if shelter was to hand, save in most favourable weather conditions, and this can be a most useful time-saver in modelling terms!

The last view, taken at Blea Moor in 1938 shows how, even without the presence of a station, certain company features are often distinctive. In this case it is the water tank, water column, signal box and buffer stop design which say 'Midland' (*J. H. Wright — courtesy NRM (2), Norman Wilkinson*).

The high speed electrics from Euston are still travelling the old LNWR 'Premier Line' and the HSTs are still very much running along the route of the GWR, MR, GN, NE and NB Railways. It is up to the modeller to identify the distinguishing marks of the railway of his choice. It may be the signal box design or the platform fencing. It may be the station furniture or buffer stop design. It may even be a fondness for a particular disposition of tracks. But it will be something quite distinctive and peculiar to that railway. For example, if I was modelling the Furness Railway I would probably feel disposed to start by making a dozen or so platform seats of that distinctive type where, in the end supports, a squirrel can be seen eating a bunch of grapes! Whatever it is, it is essential in creating atmosphere for the railway.

This gives us two thirds of the mix — the 'where' and 'which railway' but before proceeding further it as well to consider some of the possible difficulties, two or three of which will probably have sprung to mind by time. Firstly there could be a hopeless incompatibility between the desired 'geography' and the favourite railway. For example, if your liking is for rugged mountain country with trains from the Great Northern Railway then you have a difficulty and it is as well to face up to it squarely. One or other of the themes may have to be modified and since, for most modellers, I guess the choice of railway is given rather more weight than the setting, the latter may need to be adjusted. In this example offered, some sort of compromise might be found where the GNR penetrated the valleys of the old West Riding — but the opportunity for operating East Coast main line trains would have to be forgone — and so it goes on.

The second problem relates to the richness of choice available in prototype railway terms. Few of us are totally wedded to one railway to the exclusion of all others and it is frequently impossible to reconcile all our favourites. The most extreme case known to the author was that of a friend who wished to have a joint Midland and Highland system. Suggesting the LMS period was no use since he wanted pre-1923 models. The problem was never resolved and the layout was never built. I am sure there's a moral there somewhere — but there are also solutions at hand, so despair not!

A third factor might be that of space avail-

Plate 31 This was an early attempt to capture some 'Midland' flavour at 'Marthwaite'. The architecture helps but the platform fencing was wrong (later rectified), as were the gas lamps. The platform is probably too 'busy' and the unyielding eye of the camera reveals further 'horrors' like the lack of track ballast and the less than adequately modelled window detail of the buildings — but at least I had a dry stone boundary wall! (*Jim Russell*).

31

32

Plate 32 This picture was taken in 1963 to illustrate the locomotive depot at 'Marthwaite' as first built, but serves to illustrate, to some extent, the effect of putting inappropriate locomotives in the scene. The GWR 4–4–0 'Gooch' belonged to Jim Russell and the 'Caley' tank was mine. The idea was to suggest visiting engines to part of the Midland system but only the water tower really convinces. The engine shed is not quite Midland enough (albeit based on Hellifield) and the coal stage and water column are too self-evidently commercial products of the day (*Jim Russell*).

33

Plates 33 to 35 The 'when' factor in model railway terms can best be established by careful study of contemporary pictures — see also Chapter 5. These three pictures attempt to point up some of the clues to be followed up, and I have chosen non-Settle/Carlisle examples for a change.

The first picture is of Portland Old Station and the indicators of period are fairly clear. The building still looks quite new — certainly less weathered than it would in, say the 1950s — and the forecourt is clearly loose gravel, turning into mud, ie, long before the days of widespread adoption of tarmac or bitumen surfaces. There is no sign at all of mechanised road transport and the costumes of the few people in the picture are roughly turn of the century. The picture was, in fact taken on April 21 1904.

Similar analysis of the undated view of Bingley station (Plate 34) also suggests a turn of century scene. There are a few Midland trademarks but the most valuable information here is the costume detail and platform advertising, a point also brought out in Plate 35, taken at Millers Dale station in LMS days. Here, of course, one has some trains to help out and a prominent company name inscribed over the advertisement hoarding. However, the LMS lasted for 25 years so this does not get us very far. Closer examination of the two engines reveals that they are both painted in the post-1927 livery and the 4–4–0 Compound on the left displays a front shed plate of a type superseded in 1935 so we can assume the early 1930s, probably accurate enough for most people who would wish to use such a picture to help their modelling (*NRM(2), F.W. Shuttleworth collection*).

able. This has always been my own particular headache. Even if you have resolved the geography with the railway, the space available may not permit the development of a satisfying scene — so one is back to the thinking stage again. Questions such as scale and layout type then begin to raise their heads and this is where the choice of prototype and type of model tend to get mixed together. I shall return to this theme later. However, assuming that the combination of setting plus company has been adequately resolved (at least for planning purposes), we can now examine the question of time.

This is probably the first time at which the locomotive and trains begin to assume any significance at all — and then not overmuch! In fact, I would go so far as to say that the test of whether or not a model railway has atmosphere is the extent to which it can stand inspection without any trains in view. If so, then even if trains of the wrong company or period should happen to put in an appearance, they will merely look like 'foreign visitors'. However, it is abundantly clear that the design and liveries of the locomotives and rolling stock do much to suggest the historic period represented and, after all, this is what we are supposed to be modelling; so it behoves us to try and match the trains to the period by correct choice of prototype, correct livery and so forth. There are other aspects of the subject which should not be forgotten, however. Road vehicle design is very evocative of period as are the costumes of the human population, if made properly. Modern buildings should not appear in an Edwardian setting and the appropriate typeface of station signs and advertisement hoardings should be chosen. Even the street lamps are worth more than a cursory thought.

By now it will be apparent that I consider the preliminary thinking process to be almost as important as the actual building of the model. This is because I wasted so much time in the early days and resolved not to let this happen again. The point is that thinking through the problem can do wonders to clear the mind of non-essentials and thus prevent time being wasted on building or acquiring unnecessary or irrelevant items. Of course, one must be aware of a tendency to regard the planning as an end in itself — that way lies the road to permanent 'armchair' modelling! The same sort of logic can be applied to the question of layout type and models to be attempted so let me now turn to this area.

The modelling implications

In building railway models there are two main areas, the layout itself and the nature of the vehicles, stock, buildings, etc, to feature on it. They cannot be wholly separated but it does help to try.

While the modeller has been resolving the 'Where, which and when' aspects already considered, he may well have been developing ideas of the kind of layout most likely to fulfil his wishes. Setting aside space considerations for the moment, there are not many basic types of layout to consider. Essentially there is the choice of 'end to end' versus 'continuous circuit', allied to the matter of authentic operation as opposed to the demonstration running of period trains. In one sense, the end to end approach goes with prototypical operation and the continuous circuit lends itself to demonstration running but the two are by no means mutually exclusive. In an ideal world, we might prefer both options and my most recent layouts have tried to combine these two elements — but if the choice is 'either, or', then the modeller would be well advised to consider carefully his dominant preferences.

It is at this point that the site and space constraints should properly come into their own for the first time. Speaking personally, there is nothing more daunting than an empty drawing board with a site plan outlined thereon unless you, as modeller, have already developed some pretty clear ideas as to what should be the nature of the finished product. It is a moot point whether the scale of the model should take preference over the scope of the layout. The accepted wisdom of '"N" Gauge for a box room' or 'Gauge "1" for a tennis court' only holds true in the very basic sense. Sometimes, it is true, only one scale seems to be appropriate (usually one of the smaller scales chosen when faced with a constricted site) but it is often worthwhile to consider the options of different scales at the planning stage and indulge in some lateral thinking before committing yourself irrevocably.

To give a personal example, my first Settle–Carlisle models were all in 4 mm scale, starting with 'Marthwaite' (end to end), followed by 'Garsdale Road' (small, basic continuous circuit) and finally the 'Little Long Drag' — a 36 ft × 16 ft blockbuster! I had always assumed 'the bigger the better' to get the spacious effect I wanted and there is no doubt that the final layout was very spacious and looked well — but somehow it did not seem to fulfil my wishes quite as much as the earlier ones had done and I couldn't think why. I think, perhaps, that its sheer size had reduced its 'personality' compared with the earlier efforts.

It finally dawned on me that I had possibly trapped myself into a dangerously 4 mm scale way of thinking and it was only when I considered the possibility of the other scales that I resolved the problem. I chose 7 mm scale but, under different circumstances, it might just as easily have been N Gauge. Funnily enough, when I moved away from my 36 ft × 16 ft site in 1981, the space available in the new house seemed more suited to the 4 mm approach and it took 12–18 months before I could arrive at a satisfactory solution in 7 mm scale. However, the effort was worthwhile and the final scheme which did emerge promises to be as fulfilling as any I have devised so far. So, before making any irrevocable steps, give at least a passing thought to the various scale options. On the other hand, if one particular scale is dominant in your wishes, then something else may have to be sacrificed.

The next stage in the preliminaries is to resolve, as best possible, the question of the overall character of the layout in terms of balance. Are trains to dominate or is the landscape to be the main feature? Are models to be made, or are they to be bought in? If scratchbuilding is your metier, then the sheer quantity factor may be less than if ready to run equipment is chosen. One has to assess one's own model making abilities against the availability of components from

Plate 36 By the time 'Garsdale Road' was built (1968–70), I like to think I had become more discerning and I was reasonably satisfied that the overall effect spelt 'Midland', even without trains present. This picture shows Midland architecture, station nameboards, buffer stops, water tanks and columns and even facsimile trespass notices — too small to read in this view. The telegraph poles were of the MR 'double post' type but the upper quadrant signals were a bit premature for a scene supposedly in the late 1930s — although at least they suggest the post-Midland period. One never stops learning in this hobby and it is important to be self-critical when it comes to matters over which one has some control. Thus, I have to admit that the platform lamps were still not correct even though they were the proper colour (*Roy Anderson*).

36

the trade and it is no good being dishonest in one's assessment of one's own talents. There is so much good quality equipment available for sale at the present time that hand building is no longer as essential as, say, 20 years ago. The fact that some of us still opt for scratch-building is now more a matter of choice than necessity — and I am quite certain that if my model making did not match my wishes in terms of accuracy and authenticity then I would feel obliged to re-assess the whole problem.

Thus, in planning a layout to meet the various objectives discussed above, quite a lot of thinking has to be done. Ideas must be formulated, constraints acknowledged (and observed) and a fairly ruthless assessment made of the relative importance of the various desirable features — not to mention an honest appreciation on the modeller's part of the extent to which he or she feels able to carry through the project to completion in terms of both time and skill. All in all, this is quite a lot to think about and I have found it useful to do my thinking with a notepad and pencil in hand in order to jot down ideas as they emerge.

All my layouts since 1962 have been planned with these principles in mind and, although never deliberately designed to do so, gave me experience in a considerable variety of layout concepts, all of which could be put to good use in designing the next one as circumstances forced changes. They taught me that there is no perfect solution to what is in essence an impossible task — that of condensing the full size railway into the confines of a domestic environment — but that much can be achieved provided you tackle the subject fairly logically; and logic demands that we start with some clearly defined objectives.

Chapter 3

Setting the objectives and isolating the essentials

'Begin at the beginning and go on until you come to the end — and then stop'
Lewis Carroll, *Through the Looking Glass*

When the White King addressed the above remarks to Alice he cannot have had model railways in mind — but then he *was* living in a Looking Glass world! The problem with model railways is that we often seem to enter the field somewhere in the middle and rapidly discover that our consequential thoughts tend to head off happily in several different directions from the point of entry until they eventually form a closed circle of arguments — any one of which seems to offer a useful beginning but none of which really delivers the goods. So we oft times end up either being disappointed with our efforts or, worse still, doing nothing at all.

Let me explain a fairly familiar sequence of events, well known to me. Take a typical model railway show at which there may well be a layout which particularly appeals — for whatever reason. We resolve to do something similar so back home we go, inspiration renewed, and get out the drawing board, note book or what have you. Before long we realise that to get a layout like our exemplar, we need to know more about the railway itself, so research enters the picture — and we have no idea where to start. Or we discover that most of the models were scratch-built and that we have neither the detailed knowledge of the prototype nor the skill to do likewise. Alternatively we find out that the space available to us is not sufficiently similar or that the time required to make the model will be more than we can honestly spare. Where did we go wrong? Mr 'X' has done it so why can't we? The answer is devastatingly simple — we were starting in the wrong way by, in effect, wishing to make a model of somebody else's model!

This is, of course, very flattering to the original modeller whose layout proved such a spur to the imagination; but, short of slavishly copying another person's work — to my mind a pretty unimaginative thing to do — the best we can gain from other modellers is ideas and knowledge. These can then be worked upon by ourselves and modified to suit our own wishes, skills and experience. There are many other similar ways of going wrong at the outset and the only real beginning is for the modeller to accept that he must in the end create his own model railway and not copy or be over influenced by someone else. Once this notion has taken hold, not only can we draw many fruitful ideas from other modellers but we also save ourselves much time and effort.

The other trap lying in wait for the unwary is that helpful chap who urges you to 'get something running' as soon as possible! He means well because it is a very strong-minded modeller who does not want to see his models working. Moreover, it can be a positive disincentive to progress if you can't see some sort of mobility fairly soon; but don't rush in too quickly — this was the mistake I fell into in the 1950s. All I wanted to do was see the trains run and I never gave much thought to the overall effect created. Not surprisingly no decent effect was created — how could it be with GWR, LMS, LNER, BR and American HO all mixed up together! However, if you are prepared to think through the overall objectives first then there is no reason why the layout cannot be planned and built to have some trains operating quite early on. There is no mystery about it — just a willingness to think.

37

I would submit that it is vital that the modeller sets his objectives and priorities properly and tries to determine the real essentials which his model will hopefully display. To illustrate what I mean, I give below a very comprehensive list of desiderata which I have always had in mind since I started modelling the Settle-Carlisle. At this

Plates 37 and 38 These two views of 'Marthwaite' from more or less the same viewpoint are intended to show how the trackwork was changed between the first and last stages of the layout. The actual track as such was not altered, but as years progressed ballast was added and an attempt made to differentiate between the properly ballasted main line and half-buried lines to the locomotive depot and goods yard. From the beginning I had adopted quite generous turnouts and fine section rail in order to get the 'spidery' look of the prototype and this was always apparent. However, the scenic follow-up was not very effective in Plate 37 and I consider the second view to have a much more authentic feel to it — even the somewhat over-scale point tie-bars are less obtrusive. Remember, this layout was built 20 years ago before the availability of components which today help out in this respect (*Jim Russell, D. Jenkinson*).

38

39

Plates 39 and 40 I have always contended that consistency of standards and striking the right balance are more critical than slavish adherence to the last 0.1 mm of dimensional accuracy. These two pictures attempt to show how this was achieved at 'Marthwaite'. Plate 39 shows the engine shed and water tower of the first scheme, along with all the unballasted track. The second view, of the later development, shows how a more spacious effect was immediately created in the same amount of space by utilising much smaller structures, combined with more attention to some of the details — eg, the telegraph poles and bracket signal.

By this time I had put together a somewhat more appropriate mix of locomotives and stock and begun to display some of them in slightly weathered condition rather than all 'ex-works' as in the first scene. Correct liveries too, in the form of accurate lettering and numbering, had begun to appear and altogether, a much more harmonious ensemble was created. Even the commercial water crane did not seem too bad the second time round! (*D. Jenkinson*).

40

stage the list is no more than a statement of wishes, and is not set out in any order of importance or priority. Essentially the guiding principle was that the end product should be a recognisably 'scale' model railway which fulfilled most if not all of my self-imposed criteria:

a) As nearly as possible, correct appearance of track — thus fine scale not coarse. (In my case I chose EM Gauge in 4 mm scale and '0' Fine to 32 mm gauge in my 7 mm venture.)

b) Consistent standards throughout — ie authentic buildings as important as authentic rolling stock and equal care to be devoted to all aspects.

c) Correct station proportions as far as possible — ie, no unacceptable foreshortening of station length.

d) Correct balance between scenery and railway.

e) Main line, scale length trains to be operated.

f) More than adequate hidden storage capacity for the trains.

g) Maximum curve radius possible and never below 3 ft (in 4 mm) or 5–6 ft in 7 mm scale, even where not seen. Visible curves to be as gentle as possible.

h) Prototypical working to be possible in all aspects — ie, essentially end to end working regardless of layout plan.

j) Continuous running to be possible for testing and demonstration.

k) A branch line to be incorporated for added interest, including the main line junction.

l) All complex areas to be readily accessible — ie, no hidden turnouts.

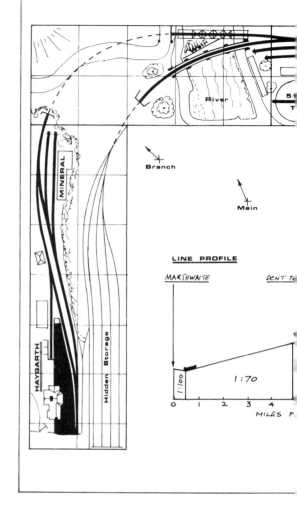

LINE PROFILE

41

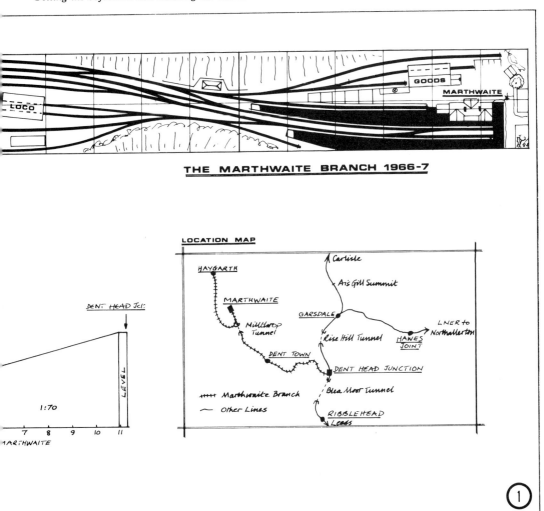

THE MARTHWAITE BRANCH 1966-7

LOCATION MAP

Fig 1 *The Marthwaite Branch* 'Marthwaite' was designed as a first attempt to produce a layout to finer scale standards and give it a believable story line. It went through two major rebuilds before reaching the form shown in this drawing. Originally there was no river and the positions of Haygarth and the storage sidings were transposed. The wish to exhibit the railway caused most of the changes; while the size of the layout was determined by the fact that it lived for most of the time in the largest (and coldest!) room in the house — along one wall and down part of another. The rest of the room had to continue to function as a bedroom.

Overall, it was a little too cramped, even when I had installed both smaller locomotive and goods sheds — and the traffic was really too intensive (prototypically) in its final years. Yet the overall size was by no means the smallest 'terminus to fiddle yard' scheme ever devised and it made me appreciate, for the first time, just how much space was needed, even for a simple scheme. The scale of the grid squares on the drawing denotes 12 in in 4 mm scale.

Plate 41 Given the smaller size of the replacement engine shed and water tower at 'Marthwaite', it became possible to envisage the place as a small country terminus with strong Midland characteristics rather than as a town with ideas above its status. This view has no real Settle and Carlisle overtones but the combination of Kirtley 0–6–0 and a more balanced grouping of authentic models of real buildings was quite pleasing. I rather think that the GWR 4–4–0 (Plate 32) would have looked like a quite genuine 'foreign' visitor this time (*D. Jenkinson*).

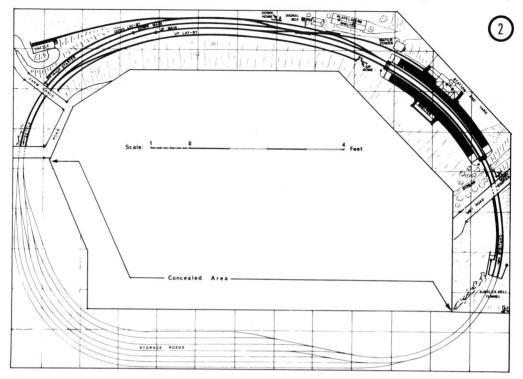

Fig 2 *Garsdale Road and Dent* 'Garsdale Road' was

m) An open stretch of main line without stations.

n) Stations to be visually separated — ie, no mythical 'split levels' to explain the proximity of two different locations!

o) The whole concept to present a theme which, even if imaginary, represents a feasible prototype situation.

p) The scheme to allow a gradual build-up with some form of operation possible at an early stage.

q) The whole thing to suggest 'Settle-Carlisle' even when nothing is happening.

r) A fairly ruthless approach to the question of 'period chosen' and 'foreign' invaders.

This is a pretty formidable list — almost a counsel of perfection, in fact. The question of compromise is considered later but suffice to say at this point that all model railways are a compromise. From the beginning we have to accept the utter impossibility of modelling every facet of the real scene. Nobody has done it yet and I doubt they ever will.

A very likely situation is that having evolved a suitable set of ideals to be aimed for, we will find that site and other constraints make it impossible to design a layout which includes them all. It is then that we need to isolate the essentials from our own personal

Fig 2 *Garsdale Road and Dent* 'Garsdale Road' was also designed against a considerable space constraint and I have thought it helpful to include a drawing of the real life Dent as well. Both drawings are overlayed with squares representing 12 in in 4 mm scale and these immediately reveal just how much compromise was needed in the modelled form. For this reason I gave the model a different name.

As a layout, it was, all things considered, rather more convincing than 'Marthwaite' — in spite of the considerable compression of both length and width, not to mention the over sharp curves related to the real thing. It is interesting to realise that even had I built the layout in 'N' Gauge in precisely the same space, the curve radii would still have been far too severe, even though scale length could, just, have been obtained. As with 'Marthwaite', this layout too was instrumental in my growing obsession with getting more length available in which to make a convincing model.

viewpoint and assign some sort of priorities to the list. It is no easy task and I would not presume to tell anyone which item should be top of the agenda or first to be discarded — but faced with the task of choosing, the modeller must have some ideas which are pre-eminently important — the essentials as far as he is concerned.

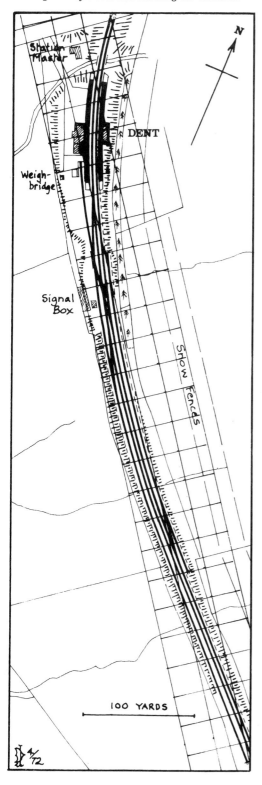

It may be useful at this stage to consider how my own models have fulfilled my own objectives — at least down to the time of writing (1984). My first effort, 'Marthwaite' in EM Gauge, was built and modified during 1962–67 when space constraint was at its most critical. I append a drawing (Fig 1) of the layout in its final and most satisfactory form. From the outset, many of my long term wishes were put 'on ice' — because the 'main line' theme had to be sacrificed. I therefore chose the branch terminus to fiddle-yard solution but wrote its 'history' based on a real junction location, notionally at Dent Head and timed the trains on the layout to 'fit' the main line.

The inspiration for the track layout came from Grassington, the nearest suitable MR terminus to my chosen route. I reversed the plan, mirror image fashion, to suit the site constraints and equipped the layout with a full array of S & C buildings plus a loco depot. The problem was that Marthwaite represented a larger place than Grassington with more traffic — yet the reality was that Grassington sprawled around and Marthwaite had to be confined to about 14–15 ft × 2 ft. I leave it to readers to judge how far it came to realising the ideal.

In the end, Marthwaite more or less fulfilled my criteria (a) (b) (c) (d) (g) (h) (k) (l) and (o) — but most of the others were shelved or ignored. I cannot in honesty comment as to its overall success, but it seemed to be well enough received. My friends and I had a lot of fun with it and it was with a real sense of regret that I had to close the line in 1967. By now it had grown a sort of 'personality' and had become quite well known in the North of England. But I was not wholly satisfied. It had become too busy (in traffic terms) and was physically too constricted for the traffic pattern we operated. In other words, I was getting close to the believability margin — and it showed.

The second attempt during 1967–72 'Garsdale Road', again in EM Gauge, was devised to meet some of the objectives which had been set aside with 'Marthwaite' and again had to cope with considerable space constraints. The site available (13 ft × 9 ft) just permitted a continuous circuit and I reckon that this time it fulfilled conditions (a) to (e), (g) (just!), (h) (j) (l) (o) and (q). In other words it was getting closer than Marthwaite and has had numerous imitators since — notably 'Heckmondwike' built to

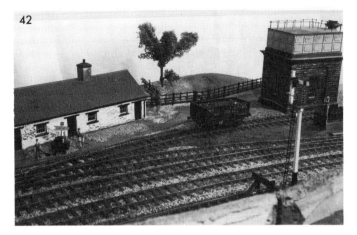

Plate 42 'Garsdale Road', like 'Marthwaite', was built to considerable size constraints but this forced a very simple track plan. In consequence, I felt it worthwhile trying to improve the trackwork and I always felt that this was one of the better features of the layout. This picture was taken to see whether the hard labour was worth while when the line was photographed and I feel that it was. It is, perhaps worth mentioning that the front to back dimension of this scene was only 18 in and this presented quite a problem in terms of scenic development (*Roy Anderson*).

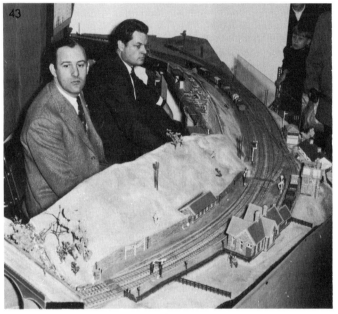

Plate 43 This is the only picture ever taken to show the whole length of either of the first two EM layouts. It shows 'Garsdale Road' on its one and only expedition to the Mecca of model-railways — Central Hall Westminster in 1970. I moved north a few months later. Essentially, the picture demonstrates the real difficulty in presenting a limited space version of a spacious prototype and the real human figures reveal only too clearly how small it was. There really was no space to develop the wild hilly nature of the real Settle and Carlisle and this, above all strengthened the resolve to improve matters (*D. Jenkinson collection*).

18.83 mm gauge by the Scalefour Society. However, if one compares 'Garsdale Road' (Fig 2a) with the real station at Dent (Fig 2b) and analyses the scale equivalences and overall character, then the layout although acceptable was again beginning to push at the margins of credibility. What I needed, I thought, was more and more space. Real railways occupy a lot of room and it seemed that I needed to as well.

Changes of occupation and residence during 1971–73 gave the chance I thought I needed — the opportunity to build a large shed to house the 'Dream' layout. By now I had amassed quite a collection of models, learned a lot about the Settle and Carlisle and

thought I knew what was needed. Thus began the building of 'The Little Long Drag' — scale length trains, full length stations — the lot! Referring to my list of criteria, all were included — and for the first time in my modelling life I could actually afford to build it. The general scheme adopted is shown in Fig 3 and, hidden curve radii excepted, there was little or no compromise. I even managed to incorporate 'Garsdale Road' in the scheme but when I realised, around 1975–76, that the layout had been essentially complete for almost two years and had only once been operated properly after completion, I felt that something had gone wrong.

Even now, some ten years after building it,

I'm not sure why it didn't satisfy me. Perhaps it was too big for one man to both develop and maintain; but it caused me to think quite furiously. Was I wrong after all? Had my criteria been wrong? Was I no longer interested in models? Had I become jaded? It may have been a bit of all these but essentially it had lost its 'fun' element. I had built a layout which seemed to fulfil all my objectives but it lacked the one thing that 'Marthwaite' and 'Garsdale Road' had both possessed — the element of pleasure. It became much more like the Ancient Mariner's albatross round my neck. I couldn't actually enjoy the layout because of the amount of work it seemed to represent — so I ignored it.

I finally came round to applying myself to the problem and concluded that, in their way, both 'Marthwaite' and 'Garsdale Road' had been better, for all their failings, because they were manageable single handed. Neither of them fulfilled all my criteria but it did occur to me that maybe a simple continuous circuit with but one passing station of relatively modest proportions and a terminus just a bit more pretentious than Marthwaite might combine the features I wanted.

This seemed a very modest ambition in a 36 ft × 16 ft shed until I thought of the scale factor. Once I had cleared my head of the grandiose 4 mm scale ideas I could then look at the very positive virtues of a larger scale — better running, more accurate appearance and so on. Consequently, my 7 mm ventures have gone back to something akin to the 'Marthwaite'/'Garsdale Road' degree of complexity but with the advantages of the

44

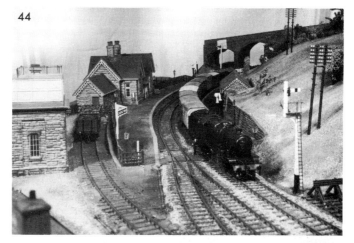

45

Plates 44 and 45 For all its smallness, 'Garsdale Road' photographed quite well in medium or close-up during its portable days and Plate 44 gives little indication of the space limitations only too obvious in the previous view. However, when it was finally integrated in the 'Little Long Drag' scheme it was possible to remedy matters and it became vastly more convincing in my eyes — even the curve radius through the platforms did not seem quite so awfully sharp. The second picture shows it in the more spacious surrounds of its final site and, with hindsight, I rather suspect that had I managed to discipline myself to keep the rest of this scheme at this degree of simplicity, it might well have survived until my forced house move of the early 1980s.

For some reason I forgot to put the buildings onto the scene for the picture to be taken and did not notice the fact until the prints were sent back! (*Roy Anderson, Ron Prattley*).

greater solidity, reliability and running quality of 7 mm scale — a fact which I had always acknowledged but could never recon-cile with my desire for space, space and more space.

Fig 4 shows the first 7 mm scheme to be

Fig 3 *The 'Little Long Drag'* This layout was the third and final 4 mm scale EM gauge attempt at the Settle-Carlisle theme. As usual, the grid squares represent 12 in in 4 mm scale so the site was roughly half a scale mile long. Such lavish space arose because in 1972–73 I was, for the first and last time in my life, in possession of a big enough garden in which to erect a large shed.

In spite of its size, the main line was completely operational in terms of trackwork and control systems by 1974 and the branch had got as far as the tunnel mouth at Kendal before activity ceased. Kendal itself was never built, partly because I was not too convinced that the track plan was correct (too complex?) and by then, more general doubts were setting in. With the exception of the platform curve through 'Garsdale Road' there was really very little in the way of compromise in the visible areas and the trains looked superb, especially when I had completed the main hill masses. I think it was simply that I had made it too big for single-handed operation, save for 'tail chasing'; whereas with its two predecessors it was possible to operate prototypically with just one person at the controls.

Even now, while re-drawing the plan for this book, I remain conscious that in many respects, this layout represented my ideal concept . . . but I now know that there are practical limits to what should be attempted by those who are still engaged in a full-time working career. The 'Little Long Drag' exceeded those limits.

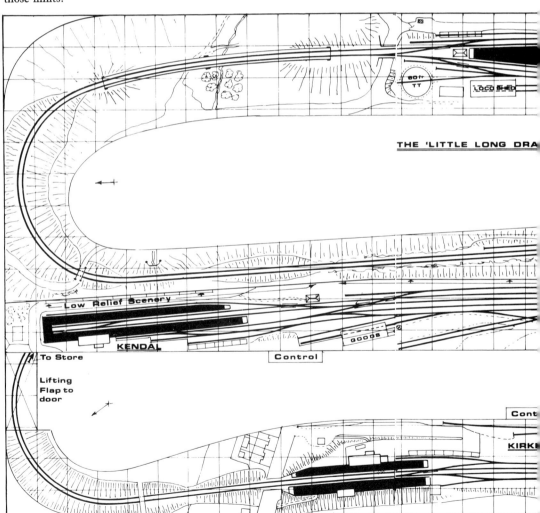

tackled in the 36 ft × 16 ft shed. It was equivalent to 20 ft × 9ft in 4 mm scale so was not exactly small. It worked beautifully for some two years but when it was about half-complete, outside considerations forced me to move house. This was somewhat frustrating but, when I finally came up with a suitable plan for my new house — in a complex of inter-connected basement cellars plus a continuous circuit making use of a low-level garden patio — I found that schematically I could not improve upon the basic concept and so, at last, I feel that I may have achieved a suitable middle-way.

Curiously, events have caused me to go to larger scale in order to keep up the momentum. Had my site possibilities gone the other way, I hope that I would have had the courage to reduce the scale. For example, my 13 ft × 9 ft site for 'Garsdale Road' might have a better prospect in N Gauge — but I never considered it at the time!

So, in concluding my remarks on isolating the essentials and based on experience I would add three more vital points, quite apart from the question of choice of scale:

a) Keep it as simple as possible, consistent with your wishes.

b) Keep it manageable single handed (unless you have a permanent clutch of helpers).

c) Make sure it will be fun — perhaps the most important of all.

My current (1983 onwards) project is my fifth attempt at producing a layout inspired by the Settle-Carlisle and I think it will be the

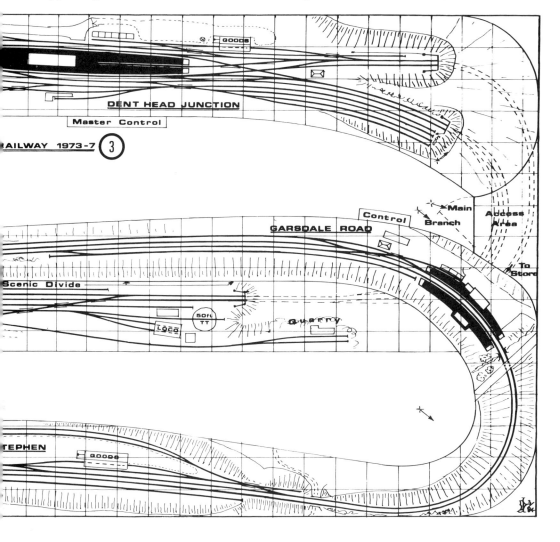

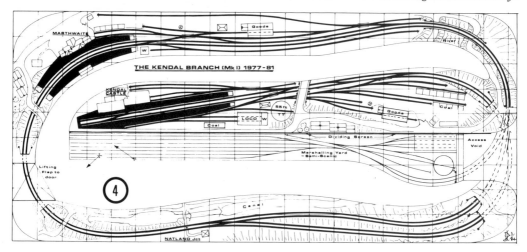

Fig 4 *The Kendal Branch (Mk I)* This plan represents the first Gauge 'O' attempt and, when compared with Fig 3, gives a very clear indication of the difference in scope, given the same floor area, between 4 mm and 7 mm scales. To maintain consistency with the other track plans, however, I have still given it a grid of 12 in squares in *4 mm* scale. In this scale it would just about fit into a longish single garage (provided the car was left outside!) although it might need slight adjustment to widen the access wells between the modelled areas.

This layout was really splendidly reliable, fully justifying the change of scale, and I can only remember one derailment (my fault!) in more than two years. The only slightly awkward feature was the concealed double junction and the minimum radius reverse curve at the entry to the storage sidings. In this latter respect, I adopted what a friend of mine has referred to as the 'full frontal' approach. In other words I made no attempt to hide the storage sidings but merely screened them from Kendal. Had it reached completion I would have made the area mildly scenic and added the locomotive depot (as drawn) to house the spare engines and give visitors plenty to look at between trains.

It was quite a wrench to have to abandon this one when it was beginning to get really interesting, but there was no way it would fit the new site (Fig 16) after my house move in 1981. I could and did, however, draw some consolation from the fact that the main portion of the through station was donated to the National Railway Museum (to form the central feature of the museum's 7 mm scale display layout) where it can be seen in operation every day.

most satisfying. It will not be as simple as 'Marthwaite' or 'Garsdale Road'. it will not look as spacious as the 'Little Long Drag' nor will it be as straightforward to build as the first 7 mm attempt; but I think it will combine, better than all of the others, those essential elements which most appeal to me. The most encouraging sign is that, even before a foot of track was laid, the concept had begun to develop a personality; and that sensation had not happened since 'Garsdale Road' was on the drawing board. I have used this final scheme to exemplify the various themes in Chapters 6 and 7, so the plan of it does not appear in this section. It has taken me 20 years — even after deciding to base my modelling on the Settle–Carlisle — to arrive at a final scheme which, hopefully, I will enjoy and which will outlast its predecessors. With hindsight I should not perhaps have taken so long; but I hope that what I have to

say in the rest of this book will help others to shorten the process — and don't worry too much if you don't get it right the first time. In spite of all I have said, there is great pleasure in 'starting anew' provided we learn from our experiences. I have thoroughly enjoyed building all four layouts — save for the latter stages of the 'Little Long Drag'. Moreover, the only modeller known to me who has consistently developed his original scheme without starting completely afresh is Peter Denny with 'Buckingham' — and he is, without doubt, a quite exceptional person in this respect and an inspiration to us all.

I have quite deliberately concentrated on what I consider to be the essential preliminary thinking processes and I hope that I have managed to convey the feeling that a degree of self-discipline has to be imposed upon an instinctive liking for railways if we are to succeed in attaining our ideal of a

Plates 46 and 47 The last two pictures show the two systems which failed to be totally completed for reasons explained in the text. I have chosen to use 'under construction' pictures, even though in both cases, these sections of each layout did get finished and both schemes were operational. The main point of the pictures is to emphasise the difference in degree of complexity between 4 mm and 7 mm scale in the same amount of space. The two engines facing the camera in each picture are in approximately the same place and the construction 'ribs' help to relate the pictures to each other. The 4 mm version is clearly of much more spacious nature, even without the scenery, but in every other respect, the 7 mm version was far more satisfactory, not least in terms of simplicity.

The confusion during the later 1970s was something of a chastening experience and made the second decade of Settle and Carlisle modelling far less rewarding in many respects than the first, even though my standards had improved in absolute terms. I only hope that this section of the book will help at least some readers not to follow suit! (*Ron Prattley*).

believable historic model. Lest this should seem to be at odds with a leisure time activity, let me remind readers that the railway itself is a highly disciplined form of transport, wherein order and rationality have, from the earliest days, been pre-eminent in the development of the systems. If our models are to succeed, they should try to reflect the order and discipline which the real railway exhibits. 'Anything goes' is rarely typical railway operating philosophy, nor should it be evident in our models. Funnily enough, however, I have found from experience that, far from putting us into a straightjacket, it is this very discipline of the railway mode of transport which offers one of the most satisfying challenges to the modeller. Yet it is possible to bend quite a lot of the rules in model form without destroying the credibility of the finished product — and it is this topic that will be considered in the next chapter.

Chapter 4

The question of compromise

'Regulations are made for the obedience of fools and the guidance of wise men.'

Anonymous RAF Staff Instructor

The model railway hobby is littered with the remnants of half finished, inconclusive models which must represent, in toto, a prodigious amount of time, money and effort; and if one is to try and analyse this state of affairs, it seems to me that why they did not satisfy was bound up, somewhere along the line, with a failure to come to terms with the question of compromise.

This chapter is concerned mainly with basic layout concepts in translating reality to a model form. Before devising any layout scheme, the modeller must realise that all model railways are a compromise in some form or other and that something will have to be sacrificed if anything is to be achieved. In a nutshell, each modeller has to decide at a personal level what is and what is not acceptable from his point of view. Again this is hardly a world-shaking observation but the writer never ceases to be surprised by the number of modellers who, to judge by their statements, seem to think that no compromise is needed — they are living in 'cloud-cuckoo' land!

The Oxford English Dictionary defines 'compromise', *inter alia* as '. . . (finding of) intermediate way between conflicting opinions, etc, *by modification of each* [authors italics]'. In model terms this means we have to decide how much 'modification' we can permit ourselves in order to find an acceptable intermediate way. The problem is that the modifications have to apply, simultaneously, to more than one aspect of the subject and at times these different aspects defy separation — but we must try. Therefore I will put my head on the block and suggest that the main areas where compro-

mise will be needed are in (*a*) The size factor; (*b*) The period factor; (*c*) The operational factor; (*d*) The 'historical believability' factor. I have not included the 'model accuracy factor' since it is my confirmed view that wherever else we may be forced to compromise, the actual appearance of our locomotives, rolling stock, buildings and the like should be as true to life as our abilities and perception will permit. This does not mean that every rivet or brake hanger needs to be modelled but it does mean, for example, that a Gresley 'A4' should suggest a real 'A4' rather than a crude commercial model tarted up with fine scale wheels and couplers. It means that a 60 ft coach should *be* a 60 ft coach, not a 54 ft vehicle repainted. It means that a station building, whether a model of a real structure or a figment of the imagination, should look as though it were capable of functioning properly and is made of the right material. It means that if we choose to model a goods shed with road access then it should look as though the road delivery vehicles really do have room to turn round, or back up to the loading bays. It means that a cattle dock should suggest that if a flock of idiot sheep get into a muddle when being driven into the cattle wagons, the loading facilities provided should be capable of dealing with the situation — and so on. As I have said, it is difficult to take each area of compromise in isolation but if the reader is willing to make his own cross-connections, I will attempt to illustrate the problems in turn.

The size factor

The size factor must be the first consideration in any railway model because we are all

Plate 48 appears on the title page.

Plates 49 and 50 It was at the ends of the layout that 'Garsdale Road' got into a bit of visual difficulty as these two pictures clearly show, both taken from the outside of the curve. Certain tricks can be adopted, such as a bridge strategically located somewhere near the point where the sharpest radius starts and this was done at both ends of the line. A few other subterfuges also help. I tried to incorporate a few eye-catching diversions such as the reverend gentleman taking photographs from the bridge, fully legible trespass signs at the platform ends and a cattle pen in front of the sharp curve to draw the eye forward from the offending curve. Even so, the wide gaps opening up between vehicles, even when viewed from a near frontal position, always irritated. A lower level viewpoint will, of course, help here (or higher baseboards) and these are all matters to take into account when designing layouts (*Brian Monaghan*).

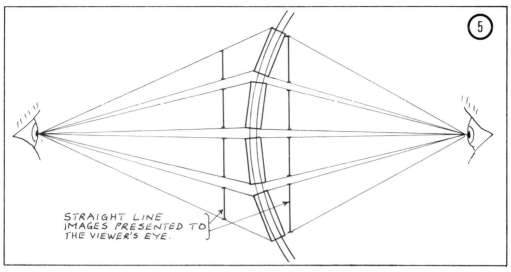

STRAIGHT LINE
IMAGES PRESENTED TO
THE VIEWER'S EYE.

Fig 5 This drawing attempts to show why it is better to view sharp curves from the 'inside'. The relative proportions of vehicles and 'gaps' is clearly much better.

constrained by the site dimensions, whatever the depth of our pockets or however skilful we may be as modellers. Therefore, above all and given a chosen scale, the model must be appropriate to the size of the site available. Only when we have decided what can and cannot be accommodated in the space on offer can we seriously consider the other factors.

The question of size resolves itself into two main areas — linear dimensions and curve radii. Let us take the latter first because it determines everything else. In reality the real railways rarely go below a 6-chain radius curve (396 ft, equivalent to 5 ft 2½ in (4 mm scale) and 9 ft 2½ in (7 mm scale)). They generally prefer more generous dimensions and on main lines, even a 10-chain curve (8 ft 8 in — 4 mm; 15 ft 4 in — 7 mm) is only considered with reluctance. Consequently, unless your site is at least 11 ft square in 4 mm scale or 19 ft square in 7 mm scale you cannot use scale radii at all. Yet between the areas defined by these two sizes (11 ft × 11 ft or 19 ft × 19 ft) are probably contained the bulk of the spaces available to most of us — spare rooms, lofts, garages etc. Moreover, many very acceptable layouts have been constructed within these dimensions without serious loss of realism. So we can reasonably conclude that curve radii can probably be compromised; the question is 'How far?' In my view this is determined by the way in which the layout is to be viewed when complete. If the layout is to be viewed from within the curve then a sharper curve radius will prove acceptable than if the view is to be from the outside of the curve; and the reason for this is entirely bound up with the attitude taken by vehicles on a curve. Viewed from the inside they close up when taking the curve, but from the outside the gap opens (Fig 5).

I would not be dogmatic on curve radii beyond stating a few general principles:

a) Use the largest curves you can manage to fit in.

b) Never work to the smallest possible radius simply because the vehicles will negotiate it.

c) Where possible try to confine sharp radii to hidden areas (see Fig 6-A).

d) It is better to have two gentle curves connected by a short straight portion than two minimum curves connected by a longer 'straight' (Fig 6-B).

e) (As a corollary to (d)) Do not be over frightened of putting turnouts on curves.

Putting this into actual dimensions, I have never worked to less than 2 ft 6 in to 3 ft radius (4 mm scale) or 5 ft 6 in (7 mm scale) except in some hidden areas, and even with this restraint I have managed to build a continuous 4 mm layout in only 13 ft × 9 ft.

The linear dimension is a much tougher proposition because here we are dealing with

Plate 51 This view, taken from the inside of the curve, demonstrates the principle explained, diagrammatically, in Fig 5. There is little doubt in my mind that the closer gaps between the vehicles go some way to compensate for the nature of the curve. Unfortunately, only the operators saw it this way round (*Roy Anderson*).

one of the really fundamental characteristics of the railway itself — its essentially 'long and thin' nature. Somehow or other we must try to capture this element and I am inclined to think that for a given area, a longer narrower site is preferable to a squareish shape. Of course we may have no choice — as indeed is my situation with the latest layout — but it is worth trying to do something even in an awkward location. In Fig 6 (C,D,E) I have sketched a few ways in which extra apparent length can be coaxed out of an awkward shape and can personally vouch for the better effect created. But at the end of the day, the modeller will eventually arrive at a linear dimension beyond which it is impos-

sible to go and it is only when this critical value is established that we can determine just what sort of feature can be modelled. Note that I say 'feature' and not 'station'. Most of us try to model a station as a first essential but perhaps we should ask ourselves whether a station is essential at all — better a nice piece of countryside with, perhaps, a small line-side quarry, all of which look believable, than to try and cram a station in where no room exists.

Let us take a typical Settle–Carlisle through station of medium size — Lazonby (Fig 7). The first thing to note is that the overall length is about four times the platform length. I have gridded the drawing to indi-

Fig 6 *Making the most of limited space* This series of drawings attempts to offer a few ways by which extra visual length can be contrived in model railway planning. Sections A to D are self-explanatory but at E I have attempted to demonstrate how even quite a short 'straight' site can be persuaded to 'expand' visually — 12 in grid squares at 4 mm scale as usual.

The trick here is, paradoxically, to increase the *width* of the layout and try to make use of the diagonal. The upper plan shows an orthodox 'terminus to storage' system which is typical of many which are built from conventional and geometrically restrictive proprietary track parts and formations. In my view it (and all like it) are pretty dull. However, the lower plan, which only involves an extra 6-9 in width, gives real scope for a railway-like approach. It does, I admit, rather presume a willingness to 'tailor-make' the track — or, at least, much of the pointwork — and it cannot 'store' any longer trains than the first scheme. However, the visual interest is present along the whole length of the site by virtue of using the diagonal as the axis of the main line and the scenic possibilities are much enhanced.

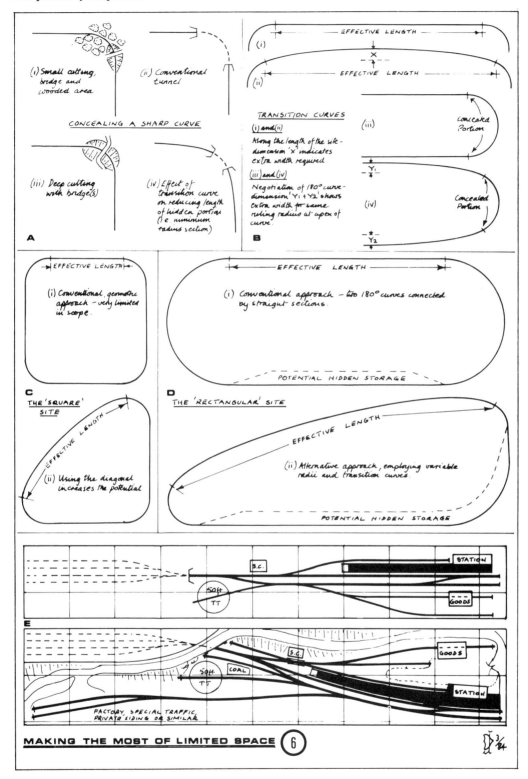

A

(i) Small cutting, bridge and wooded area

(ii) Conventional tunnel

CONCEALING A SHARP CURVE

(iii) Deep cutting with bridge(s)

(iv) Effect of transition curve on reducing length of hidden portion (i.e. minimum radius section)

B

EFFECTIVE LENGTH

(i)

EFFECTIVE LENGTH

(ii)

X

TRANSITION CURVES

(i) and (ii)

Along the length of the site - dimension 'x' indicates extra width required.

(iii) and (iv)

Negotiation of 180° curve - dimension 'Y1 + Y2' shows extra width for same ruling radius at apex of curve.

(iii)

Concealed Portion

Y1

(iv)

Concealed Portion

Y2

C

EFFECTIVE LENGTH

(i) Conventional, geometric approach - very limited in scope.

THE 'SQUARE' SITE

EFFECTIVE LENGTH

(ii) Using the diagonal increases the potential

D

EFFECTIVE LENGTH

(i) Conventional approach - two 180° curves connected by straight sections.

THE 'RECTANGULAR' SITE

POTENTIAL HIDDEN STORAGE

EFFECTIVE LENGTH

(ii) Alternative approach, employing variable radii and transition curves.

POTENTIAL HIDDEN STORAGE

E

S.C.

STATION

50ft TT

GOODS

S.C.

GOODS

50ft TT

COAL

STATION

FACTORY, SPECIAL TRAFFIC, PRIVATE SIDING OR SIMILAR

MAKING THE MOST OF LIMITED SPACE ⑥

3/84

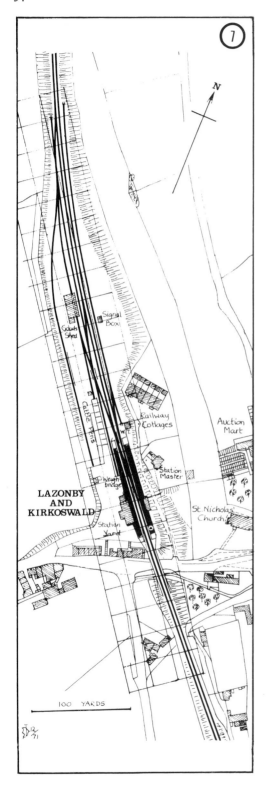

LAZONBY
AND
KIRKOSWALD

100 YARDS

Fig 7 *Lazonby Station — Settle and Carlisle line*
Lazonby, along with Armathwaite and Kirkby
Stephen (see Fig 3) were my favourite Settle-
Carlisle stations in the days when all had a full
array of features. They were so typically Midland
and so interesting in their operational potential
that were I ever forced to model but one typical
'Settle-Carlisle inspired' scene it would be based
on one of these three — as, indeed was 'Marthwaite' at Kendal (Mk I), Fig 4.

This drawing shows the real layout, overlain as
usual with a grid representing 12 in squares at
4 mm scale. Little more needs be said save to
comment that even a 20 ft x 3 ft site would not get
you much beyond the boundary fence!

Fig 8 *Essence of Lazonby* This drawing shows how
Lazonby might be reduced in length, to some
extent, for model purposes. The drawing is anno-
tated to indicate areas of compromise and, as can
be seen, totally unprototypical curves begin to
insinuate themselves at both ends. This is about as
far as I would personally be prepared to go and
still call it 'Lazonby'; but if I wanted to use the
basic track layout in a shorter or narrower location
then I would adopt the 'might have been' approach
— eg, Fig 4.

Plates 52 and 53 These two typical prototype
scenes show the sort of thing which is probably
impossible to model even in 'N' Gauge on a tennis
court! The trouble is that it is scenes like this
which frequently evoke the prototype and fire the
imagination. Take, for example, the classic view
of Shap Wells in later steam days (April 1962).
This train is 40 wagons long and with its two
locomotives stretches for almost 1,000 ft. In cases
like this it is better to admit defeat from the start
rather than be doomed to frustration.

The second picture shows Crosby Garrett
station on the Settle and Carlisle. The bridge
across the platforms was a most intriguing feature
and the main station building was augmented by
two platform shelters — all of which can be seen.
It had goods shed, cattle pens and all the other
typical features but I can see no way in which the
long straight approaches could be re-created in a
model which would fit the domestic environment.
The best solution might be to 'lift' a few ideas and
incorporate them in a 'might have been' scheme.
Yet the scene is typically 'railway' (*Gavin Wilson,
W. Hubert Foster — courtesy NRM*).

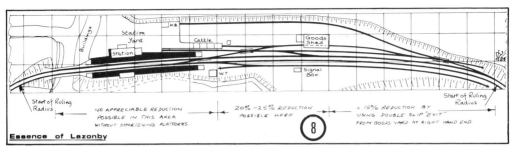

Essence of Lazonby

Start of Ruling Radius

NO APPRECIABLE REDUCTION POSSIBLE IN THIS AREA WITHOUT SHORTENING PLATFORMS

20% – 25% REDUCTION POSSIBLE HERE

c. 15% REDUCTION BY USING DOUBLE SLIP "EXIT" FROM GOODS YARD AT RIGHT HAND END

Start of Ruling Radius

Plate 54 This sort of scene offers possibilities for the limited space modeller as a substitute for a proper station. It shows the lineside quarries at Stainforth between Settle and Horton-in-Ribblesdale c 1946. The tremendous limestone face offers a suitable backscene theme and the essence of the idea should take up less space than a conventional goods yard. Disregarding stopping passenger services, it probably saw more daily shunting activities than a typical goods yard as well — and all the main line activity passed in front of the scene (*W. Hubert Foster collection — courtesy NRM*).

cate 12 in squares in 4 mm scale and we can see at a glance that the overall length scales to 20–23 ft; yet the platforms will only accommodate a 4/5 coach train. How much shorter can this layout be made without destroying the nature of the prototype? If we halve its length, then to keep things in proportion the platforms would come to 2/3 coaches long; but we cannot halve the scale of the buildings to keep the balance, so we end up with a station building two thirds the length of the platform — a patently absurd state of affairs which would present a visual horror.

I have tried (Fig 8) to produce the essence of Lazonby in as short a length as I felt could be tolerated. I have slightly tightened the pointwork by adopting somewhat less gentle turnouts and curved the approach tracks — but neither of these should go too far or else the lovely flowing nature of the prototype trackwork would begin to look toylike and, to me at all events, not very satisfactory. If this plan were combined even with minimum radius approach tracks, the length would still possibly be too great for many people. Furthermore, it is at least debateable whether or not one should go on calling it 'Lazonby' at all. It was precisely for this reason, when I

made my model based on Dent, that I gave it another name, because I felt it had gone a bit too far from reality although the result was fairly acceptable in visual terms.

Paradoxically, a terminal station handling the same or considerably more traffic than Lazonby need not necessarily take up as much room — if only because the approach tracks are confined to one end — but the modeller may not want a terminal or it could be that the chosen prototype, like the Settle–Carlisle, had no terminal stations anyway. The problems of terminus designs are considered in Chapter 6.

Reverting then to the fundamental problems of length; in my judgement it is a very difficult task indeed to compromise the length of a real station for model purposes and still retain its essential nature. As a rule of thumb I would say: 'No more than 25 per cent linear reduction and be very careful!' Consequently I believe it better to have the length available to tackle a more or less scale length reproduction before tackling a model of a real location. I did it once in 4 mm scale (Kirkby Stephen) and even with 3 ft curve radius hidden approaches (and a few non-existent cuttings to hide them) it came to

36 ft long. To be fair it did look right; but so much so as to convince me that it would not have looked right in say 25 ft of length!

Which brings this discussion fairly obviously to the next and related area of compromise.

The 'historical believability' factor

It is probably a *non-sequitur* that if we model a real station to true scale length and with high accuracy then it ought to be historically believable. I suppose that Geoff Williams' EM Gauge 'Aylesbury' layout was the first real proof of that and, in more recent years, 'Bodmin' in Scalefour. But as I have outlined above, this does pre-suppose close attention to the length factor for ultimate success.

At the same time, I do firmly believe that it is possible to use the 'based upon an idea' theme as opposed to 100 per cent authenticity and still create a totally convincing scene. The doyen of this approach was, and still is, Peter Denny with 'Buckingham'. He has had numerous imitators (including myself) but we don't always succeed in creating the end product we seek and I think the main reason for this is a lack of attention to the unwritten 'ground rules' governing this alternative approach.

The key word is 'believable' — and it almost defies adequate definition. In a sense, for a model based upon an idea to be believable, the observer has to suspend belief in the prototype reality and substitute for it the quasi-fictional reality of the miniature scene. It is not easy to achieve this switch but there are a few basic principles we can follow.

First and foremost must be a convincing story line. My good friend, Arthur Whitehead, was (and is) very fond of starting a debate on a projected layout scheme with the words: 'Just supposing . . .'; and herein lies the key. If we are to make a model of a line or station which did not really exist at all (and that is what it boils down to) then it must have some sort of economic and geographical feasibility. Fortunately, the history of Britain's railways is festooned with abandoned 'might have been' proposals and a bit of research into these can often generate ideas for models.

This is only the second time in this book that the word 'research' has been seriously mentioned — deliberately so. Research is so fundamental to good historical modelling that I have felt it desirable to devote a whole chapter to the subject. But I do not think it

worthwhile for the modeller to be diverted into the fascinating world of research until he is fairly clear in his own mind just what it is he needs to research. It can, all too easily, become an end in itself so, in consequence, I have included it fairly late in the book.

Be that as it may, we are now at the interface with research and if we are going to adopt one of the many 'might have beens' as the basis for a model — or even invent our own story line — then it must be a story which carries conviction. I said in Chapter 3 that the railway was a structured organisation and it can be stated almost categorically that no group of entrepreneurs would have built a real railway had there not been promise of traffic to justify the expense of building it. The fact that many of the unfulfilled proposals never became reality was probably due to their lack of real traffic potential, so the modeller must beware of what I call the 'geographically nonsensical' approach. It can get even more complicated when we bring in the historical period because what might have been geographically sensible in the 1850s may have become a nonsense by the late 1870s — or vice versa. That is why many railways arrived late and died early. But, of course, quite a number of marginal proposals did get built so why should not the modeller add to the list? After all, the Settle–Carlisle itself was probably the biggest geographical aberration in our railway history, save, perhaps for the London extension of the Great Central; but they were both built! At the end of this chapter I have offered a few 'might have beens' to illustrate the points I am trying to make.

The period factor

Somebody once said that 'History begins yesterday' and in railway terms it could not be more true. To those of us whose stable world of railways had begun to collapse with the nationalisation of 1948, only to be given the *coup-de-grace* by the elimination of steam 20 years later, it is almost reassuring to realise that the 'Deltics' (which, if you remember, killed off the East Coast 4–6–2s) are, in 1985, just as much an historical anachronism as LMS 'Duchesses', GWR 'Kings' and, from an earlier generation, LNWR 'Georges' and Caledonian 'Dunalastairs'. But I can't resist commenting that steam engines usually enjoyed a longer life before they had seen out their time! The

55

Plates 55 and 56 These two pictures are separated in time by some five years or more but they exemplify the point made in the text about there being certain periods when some form of visual stability was to be witnessed. The two pictures represent the early and late 1930s on the Leeds to Carlisle line at Bell Busk (near Hellifield) and Ais Gill respectively. Both show similar trains — the mid-day St Pancras to Scotland through service which carried through coaches of LNER ownership for the Edinburgh portion. The Bell Busk train is headed by a 'Patriot' Class 4-6-0 and the picture was probably taken before the Stanier 'Jubilee' (behind the Compound 4-4-0 at Ais Gill) was even built. Yet, a year or two after the Bell Busk picture was taken, these two trains with precisely the same engines and carriages and in virtually the same liveries might well have passed each other going in opposite directions. The 'Patriot' (No 5534) would by then have received a name, *E.Tootal Broadhurst*, but otherwise there would be little significant change. The train engine at Ais Gill is No 5562 *Alberta* and the Compound No 1045. This picture was taken in 1939 and all three engines were at Leeds during the later 1930s. In fact I had models of all of them in 4 mm days and could replicate the trains. There are many points of interest here, not the least being the six-wheel milk tanks at the head of the southbound train (*D. Jenkinson collection, M. W. Earley, courtesy NRM*).

56

French have a phrase for it — '*plus ça change, plus c'est la même chôse*'. (The more things change, the more they stay the same.)

What I am trying to say is that unless the modeller is prepared to be so dedicated to historical authenticity as to place his model at, say, June 16 1944, it is almost impossible for him to select any historic period without encountering problems. God willing, we enjoy this earthly life for the appointed 'three score and ten', during most of which time we are consciously reacting to the scene around us — including railways. If, as in my case, your interest in the subject has been maintained for most of your life, then it is simply not possible to pick one period for a model which has all the desired elements in it. One may well succeed in resolving the size factor, the setting of the model, and if imaginary, the 'believability' factor; but, I venture to suggest, the time factor will always trip you up. I am very fond of the LMS Railway (and its constituents) but I can't run an LNWR train on the Settle–Carlisle (much less a Highland one), nor, even if I painted them all in LMS colours, could I realistically operate an ex-Furness Railway 'Sharp-Stewart' 4–4–0 (scrapped in 1927) alongside a 'Duchess' 4–6–2 (built in 1938) or a red-painted ex-HR 'Loch' Class (all of which were black by the mid–late 1930s). Yet all three types are amongst my favourites and I have models of two of them — so what can one do?

The first point to realise is that there was not, and never will be, a time when things do not change. Sometimes it goes quickly, at other times (rarely long-lasting) there seems to be some stability; so in railway modelling terms it would be unreasonable to expect to find a period on which to base the model when nothing was likely to change. The simple solution to this dilemma like so many others, is to ignore it.

This is not to say that we cannot reach an acceptable compromise but simply to state that the modeller should not get himself too 'uptight' about the period factor. After many years of historical modelling it has occurred to me that there are three reasonably satisfying solutions to the period factor problem:

a) The purist approach — fixed year (or, more realistically a season of the year) when little or nothing of any significance actually changed.

b) The semi-purist approach — essentially as (a) but allowing for the possibility of a few out of period models to make their appearance under controlled conditions.

c) The model museum approach — wherein historical period accuracy is sacrificed to the wish to model typical items from a variety of favoured periods.

Which of these three is chosen is very much a matter of personal inclination, but it seems worthwhile examining the implications of each.

In terms of ease of decision making, the purist approach is the simple one. A time is chosen which most appropriately fits the desires of the modeller and all non-appropriate or out of period blandishments are strenuously resisted. It sounds remarkably simple and I have tried it for myself. My first two EM Gauge layouts were quite firmly based on the 1937 situation. I could have pre-group, early LMS and Stanier items all intermixed, provided I painted everything in LMS colours, and there seemed to be no problem — until I suddenly fancied a Johnson 4–2–2 and a Deeley 990 (both scrapped c 1928) and a non-streamlined 'Duchess' (built 1938 and later). Frankly, I funked it and, in a sort of wishy-washy way, temporised at the LMS c 1928-38. But, gentle reader, there was no such thing as the 'LMS c 1928-38'! Think about it for a moment and you won't need me to tell you why. This is where my own modelling stood when I abandoned 4 mm scale in 1976.

The opposite end of the spectrum is also pretty simple — the 'model museum' approach. Here, suspension of belief in time is paramount and you simply make models of trains which appeal and run them in a pleasant, sort of neutral (or should it be neutered?) setting. Why not? It is no great secret that I am employed at the National Railway Museum and, unsurprisingly, became involved (I may add, somewhat reluctantly) with the museum's model display. In this presentation we were faced with a space problem, somewhat analagous to the domestic situation, but additionally complicated by the sheer range of available models — basically pre-group to BR! We chose the 'model museum' approach, not because we *were* a museum, but because it seemed the most appropriate way of displaying the concept of 'Trains through the Ages' which was the dominant wish. It seems to have worked — provided that the observer is prepared to reconcile the broadly 1930s/1940s nature of the scenery and lineside effects with the

1900-70 characteristics of the trains which are paraded through this static scene. But it does not particularly satisfy me — and I have to say so to myself, if to no-one else!

Overall, therefore, I find myself coming down strongly in favour of the semi-purist solution. In this approach one selects the most favoured historical period and tries to develop the model around this concept. One can then, if careful, insert a few historical or geographical anachronisms. To illustrate the realisation of this approach I can only quote my own preferred solution, arrived at after some 20 years or more of experimentation. The space now available to me (after a succession of house moves already mentioned) suggested that a realistic '100 per cent main line' characteristic (my preferred choice) would not be wholly satisfactory so I was forced to adopt a 'secondary main line-cum busy branch line' solution. This went a long way towards my ideal. I could, quite reasonably, include models of somewhat ancient engines and elderly carriages and wagons, together with somewhat more modern and up-to-date items, provided I confined my attention to the c 1930 period — ie, immediately preceeding the LMS modernisation and rationalisation of the late 1930s. Consequently, my latest model plans (now in the process of realisation) envisage a setting based on the LMS of the year 1930. Some items were still bedecked in their earlier finery but austerity was (just) beginning to creep in. Thus I can have elderly red engines but a few more modern items as well; while my favoured setting (Settle–Carlisle) had not seriously entered into its terminal decline — dating in my judgement, from c 1960 onwards. The only residual problem was that of

Plate 57 I was at first tempted to put this picture in the next chapter as an example of the type of view which is so valuable in the research context. It is obviously Paddington and equally obviously the late 1930s (February 1939 in fact) but it carries a wealth of useful detail — carriage livery, dress styles and, above all, that magnificent refreshment trolley. We accept that there is no movement because we know it is a moment 'frozen in time' as it were; but, and this is the key question, should we try to model such scenes? The open door and the teapot would seem to present a few problems on an operational model railway and an attempt is made to show this in the remaining pictures in this chapter (*NRM*).

57

Plate 58 This view of Marthwaite station building was a last ditch attempt to disguise a damaged window at the York Model Railway Show of 1966 by hiding it with a window cleaner. That particular pane of glass was religiously polished for more than 72 hours! The picture also shows a pretty awful attempt at hiding the base of the building. In fact it was not until I saw this picture that I fully realised how unsightly was the gap between buildings and ground (*Brian Monaghan*).

how to reconcile this decision with my personal wish to operate both Stanier engines and pre-1923 prototypes.

In solving this dilemma, I took the example of my late and much beloved friend, Gavin Wilson. He was a great Highland-railway modeller but he loved the Stanier 'Duchesses'. So he built a model of the Highland (c 1914 I guess) in superb fidelity but (and it is an important 'but'), hidden out of sight was the 1937 *Coronation Scot* and the 1938 Royal Train and *Royal Highlander*. When he felt like it, out they came for a trip round the layout. His model always evoked the Highland (his favourite scene) but he could, from time to time, run his 'funny trains', as he called them, without destroying the realism of his basic setting.

Consequently — and given the time and opportunity — I hope to re-create a bit of the LMS c 1930, based on the Settle–Carlisle; but, out of sight, I propose to have such favourites as a Midland express of the late 1890s, the WCJS '2pm' in all its pre First World War glory (with a 'George' or 'Cardean' as its motive power), the LMS Royal Train of 1938 and a typical Settle-Carlisle express of the late 1930s. They will, in purist terms, look ridiculous, but they will please me — and that is all that really matters. I would even include a Chapelon 'Nord' 4–6–2 with a train of blue wagons-lits if I had the time or skill to build them.

The point of all this is that we should not allow ourselves to be over-influenced by others. Ultimately, the greatest satisfaction lies in doing that which pleases us — and to hell with the rest of the world! Conse-

Plate 59 This scene was a deliberate attempt to inject a humorous distraction from the sharp 'exit' curve at 'Garsdale Road'. Anyone who has ever driven in the Pennines will know the experience only too well. As a static view it comes off quite well but . . . (*Brian Monaghan*).

quently, one can think of examples in all three categories which were acceptably excellent. In purist terms one can include 'Aylesbury', 'Bodmin', 'Heckmondwike' and 'Buckingham', two of which are models of real stations at real times and two of which are 'might have beens'. In 'museum' terms, the late Alan Shackleton (coarse scale) and W. S. Norris (fine scale) came as close as anyone might wish and in the middle ground I submit that my old friend Gavin Wilson came as close as reasonably possible. The choice is yours and I am not inclined to pontificate.

The operational factor

There are two basic sorts of railway model-lers — those who like to build and/or collect models in their own right and those who like to operate them as well. A very dear friend of mine gave as her opinion that in one sense the movement of model trains destroyed the reality of the scene in that it was only the trains which moved — the people did not walk, the road vehicles did not move and the trees and grass did not wave in the wind. She

could accept the reality of the static scene — a sort of three-dimensional picture 'frozen in time' as it were — but was not totally con-vinced that the movement of the locomotives and rolling stock *only*, actually contributed to the 'believability' of the total presentation. This point of view had never occurred to me before but it seemed, on reflection, to display considerable depth of perception. There is after all something faintly absurd in wanting to see the trains move when everything else is static — think about it for a moment and you will see what I mean. Yet, taking the oppo-site view it seems an awful shame if we can make some of the models move realistically not to let them do so. So, once again, we are in the realm of compromise.

My own view, for what it is worth, is that there is little purpose in building a layout merely to enable a locomotive and its train aimlessly to orbit an otherwise static scene, however well modelled. This may, for a while, recreate a pseudo-realistic vision of a train in motion but it will not, and in the last analysis, cannot go much further. But it is possible to achieve the kind of mobility in

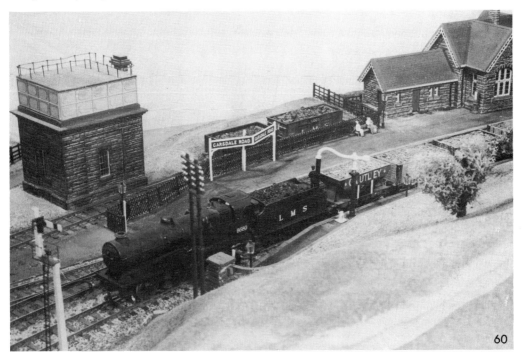

Plate 60 This picture was quite deliberately posed to show the locomotive taking water while the signal was at danger, and could not, of course, be a permanent feature of the layout. However, on the opposite platform I put a group of seated passengers and I feel this is acceptable. Thus, I find myself coming round to the view that if human figures are to be inserted onto the scene, they should be in essentially static situations. This would rule out football, tennis and even cricket matches but would not eliminate a group enjoying a drink at the pub in the open air, a farmer leaning on a gate or a fisherman having a snooze! It is a very personal matter but one which, I feel, should be given a modest degree of thought (*Roy Anderson*).

locomotives and trains which re-enacts the majority of operational characteristics of the real railway (excluding human movement) so as to create a believable scene, even allowing for the non-realistic aspects of some part of the model. To do this demands that the historical modeller knows and understands the operational nature of the real railways. In other words, the model should look as though it could be operated realistically even if we simply choose to indulge in 'tail chasing' — and, if possible, can be operated realistically as far as the movement of locomotives, rolling stock and signalling is concerned.

The nature of such operational characteristics varies from period to period. There is a world of difference between the steam age marshalling yard of the inter-war period (or the shunting of its contemporary local pick-up freight as a natural corollary) and the modern-day equivalent — likewise in pas-

senger train handling. The traditional 'old fashioned' mode of operation necessitated certain types of track layout and stock provisioning, whereas modern railway operation imposes different constraints. Furthermore, in the pre-group period, it was not uncommon for different companies to solve essentially similar operating problems by employing quite dissimilar track formations. These were sometimes forced by the site, but often were simply a reflection of a company preference for certain types of track formation (eg, the Midland's fondness for double slips and three-way turnouts). Naturally enough many of these pre-1923 preferences lasted well into the modern era before simplification and rationalisation became the order of the day.

Thus it is for the individual modeller to identify those operational characteristics (and their consequential effects upon track layout etc) which most distinguish his chosen period and railway and then incorporate them into his layout plan. To illustrate this point, it is only necessary to compare the 1930s and 1940s track layout of any busy location (eg, Euston, Kings Cross, St Pancras) with its 1980s equivalent to demonstrate the changes which have occurred — almost always in the realm of simplification. The same is equally true of more modest locations but they are far too numerous to list.

The implication of this argument is that the track layout itself is just as vital a part of the historical model as is the nature of the rolling stock to be run on it. Indeed I would go so far as to say that the desired operational characteristics of the model should be the dominant influence in the actual track plan devised, regardless of scale, period or whatever and I shall go into more detail on this subject in Chapter 6. Suffice to say at this point that this area too, presupposes on the part of the modelmaker, some sort of understanding of the prototype. To gain this

understanding demands research and unless the putative historical modeller is prepared to undertake some sort of research, then his efforts are likely to be disappointing. But it is important that the research is conducted against the background of a known requirement. Before analysing the research aspect of the subject in detail, it may be helpful to draw the threads together by looking at a few possible layout suggestions based upon the principles enumerated so far.

Some layout schemes analysed

On the next few pages I have offered a variety of layout concepts, all but the last being loosely based on the Midland Railway and/or Settle-Carlisle way of doing things. Some of them I have actually built while others were schemes worked out for possible layout sites which did not materialise. Most of them could, by suitably adaptation, serve for other prototypes, provided that the modeller was willing to write his own story-line and pos-

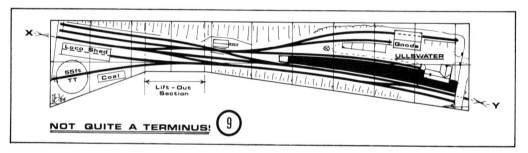

Fig 9 *Not quite a terminus!* I have often been accused by my friends of never seriously considering the truly space-starved modeller — and I suppose I must admit that I have usually been able to find at least some sort of site to work in, even in my 7 mm efforts where space is, undoubtedly, more difficult to contrive.

This plan is derived from Fig 6(E) and was worked out for the benefit of a keen 7 mm scale enthusiast friend of mine who had but 18 ft of length in which to develop a fine scale Gauge 'O' concept in his workshop — a conventional house extension of 'conservatory' style. Basically all he wanted was a simple continuous circuit with some main line pretensions and an interesting station as centrepiece. The 18 ft x 8 ft site would not permit this in 7 mm scale within its walls, but there was a prospect of building a portable 'outside' link between X and Y in the form of a simple oval. At the same time, however, it was desired to have a plan which would be capable of limited operation in bad weather and would at least look logical even if the outside option did not materialise. The conventional end to end solution shown in Fig 6(E) was not quite what was required so we started to consider a few 'just supposings'! The desired theme was LNWR c 1905 and we finally hit upon the possible linking of the Windermere branch with the Keswick to Penrith line via Troutbeck and Ullswater — single line, of course — as a sort of emergency alternative to the Shap route.

Gradients would be a bit fearsome in reality — but that never seemed to worry the LNWR — and, in model form, would serve to explain the 4-6-0s and 0-8-0s on quite small trains. The result was 'Ullswater', wherein all essential shunting can be carried out between the bridges (to stay inside the workshop!) but which, if a continuous link was added, could equally well function as a suitable passing station. The loco shed is for the banking engine and the carriage sidings are for the Ullswater-Penrith local trains. Indeed, a third operating option is a 'plug-on' storage magazine at X as an alternative to the continuous link. If this solution was adopted, it could be assumed that funds ran out when the line had reached Ullswater from the Penrith end! As usual, the grid represents 12 in squares at 4 mm scale.

sibly make some track modifications to suit his chosen period and railway. I have rarely suggested much scenic treatment — beyond recommending where tunnels etc, may be located — because I wish to concentrate here on the basic geometry of the layout itself in terms of what can and cannot be fitted into a given location. None is perfect and most could (by slight stretching or compression) be tailored to suit slightly different site dimensions — but I would not recommend reduction by more than about 10-15 per cent in most cases.

I would also make one other point. None of the schemes have been designed with commercial pointwork in mind. At the risk of sounding uncompromising, I do not believe it is possible to make a layout look as if a permanent way engineer had a hand in it solely by using standard left- and right-hand turnouts. I feel that the potential historical railway modeller is, sooner or later, going to have to face up to the making of handbuilt pointwork if his efforts are to convince. Use commercial plain track, by all means, but have a care with the pointwork.

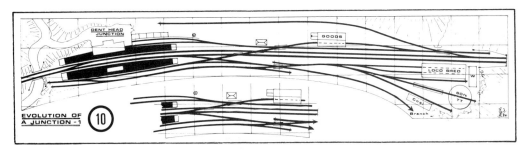

Fig 10 *Evolution of a Junction — 1* This second layout suggestion is one of my oldest ideas and embodies, in rather more space, the same ideas as Fig 9 — in other words it is a design for the man who must have a main line even if there is no room for one! It was inspired by the efforts of a gentleman I first met at about the time I had built the first 'Marthwaite' (Fig 1). This man, Norman Wilkinson, was just as infatuated with the Settle-Carlisle as myself but was quite determined to model the main line. He had no room for a terminus to storage system, let alone a continuous main line, even in 4 mm scale; so he simply built a lovely model of Settle station down the longest spare wall he could find and made no attempt to do more than create a superb representation of this one station. The main line at each end simply 'collided' with the wall, as it were — but he had achieved his bit of railway history and his efforts were published in the model journals a decade or so ago.

When I had seen Norman's layout I began to wonder if, within the same overall length as 'Marthwaite', I could build the centrepiece of the much-desired main line junction. I suppose I hoped that one day I might just get the bit of extra length needed to link it with 'Marthwaite' and it still occurs to me that if a modeller feels that one day he might get a bit more space to play with, he could do a lot worse, provided he has patience, than to build a sort of 'working diorama' as an interim step. Thus, this plan was drawn up around 1967-68 and would have been built in preference to 'Garsdale Road' had I been able so to do. In the event I had a 13 ft x 9 ft site and this would not suit.

The plan as drawn is a sort of 'marriage' between the 'Lazonby' theme along one side of the main line and the Hawes branch bay at Garsdale on the other. I have given as an inset drawing, an alternative station 'throat' which would cause a few more shunting problems but might actually look better. The plan would need another 25 per cent or so of length to allow incorporation into a continuous circuit but could, I suspect, be shortened a little. As it stands it could be shunted properly and there would not be too much difficulty in contriving some sort of 'fiddle yard' on the branch line itself.

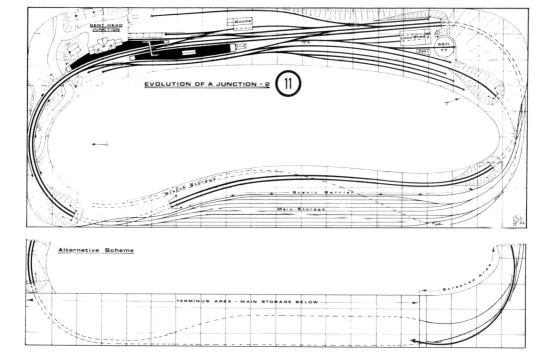

Fig 11 *Evolution of a Junction — 2* This plan is yet another 'almost but not quite' in my various house-moving activities. Essentially developed from Fig 10, it is an attempt to produce a similar concept, incorporating a continuous circuit, in rather less overall length than would be needed for Fig 10 plus approach curves. The reduction in length is achieved by staggering the junction platforms, inserting a gentle curve through the station and reducing the size of the locomotive depot. It is also possible to run directly from branch to main — at least in one direction. Overall, I think the junction layout is better in this version but the curve radius over the viaduct is a little on the sharp side.

Two possible continuations are given. The main drawing shows a way of 'hiding' the storage loops, yet permits trains to be seen for much of their transit of the opposite side of the site by allowing them to by-pass the storage. Of course, by using this cut-off, the train does inevitably become a 'tail-chaser'. The alternative idea assumes a terminus built above the main line storage allowing a facility of reasonable complexity — say about the scope of the first 'Marthwaite' (Fig 1). Indeed, this was the original idea.

When I changed to 7 mm scale, this plan was resurrected, since in Gauge 'O' terms, it was just about right for my garden shed. In the end I settled for the scheme shown in Fig 4 which gave much the same operational scope but offered more visible main line *and* a terminus — but at the cost of more pointwork and greater track complexity.

Fig 12 *Variation on a theme* This plan is an attempt to re-design Fig 11 for a shorter, wider site, making use of the principles in Fig 6(D). It was sketched out, originally, as a possible attic scheme for my new house in 7 mm scale.

Essentially, the track plan is the same as Fig 11 but the goods yard at the junction has been altered to place the sidings on the, now wider area of baseboard behind the main station. As with Fig 11 it should be possible to envisage an alternative version with a branch terminus above the main line storage.

Fig 13 *On from 'Garsdale Road'* Of all the layouts I have built to completion so far, there is no real doubt that 'Garsdale Road' was my favourite. In spite of the many reservations I have expressed about curve radii, length etc, there was something about the model which I found very satisfying. Consequently, back in the early 1970s, before the big shed became a possibility, I played around with numerous ideas designed to turn 'Garsdale Road' into the site for the junction between main line and branch. None of them came to anything but, for this book, I thought I would have another try.

I took the same site dimensions as Fig 12, some 16 ft 6 in x 10 ft in 4 mm scale and just let things happen! The end product was the appended plan. Had I decided to put my new 7 mm layout into the attic, then I think this plan might well have been tackled — or something very similar.

The story line could be anything within reason and is most certainly not tied to the Settle-Carlisle line. The main station is now presumed to be a junction between two companies, one of which operates the main line and the other the single track system. The hidden pointwork allows either of the two routes to be fed from the same set of storage roads out of sight of the viewer. The simple terminus serves to conceal this subterfuge and could be made even more 'basic' than I have drawn it. It is connected to the main line by the double junction at the left hand end of the site. The scheme is essentially end to end (storage roads to terminus) but with the assumption that quite a lot of the traffic from the storage roads would reverse direction at the junction and go back to the storage roads via the 'other company's' route. It would, in

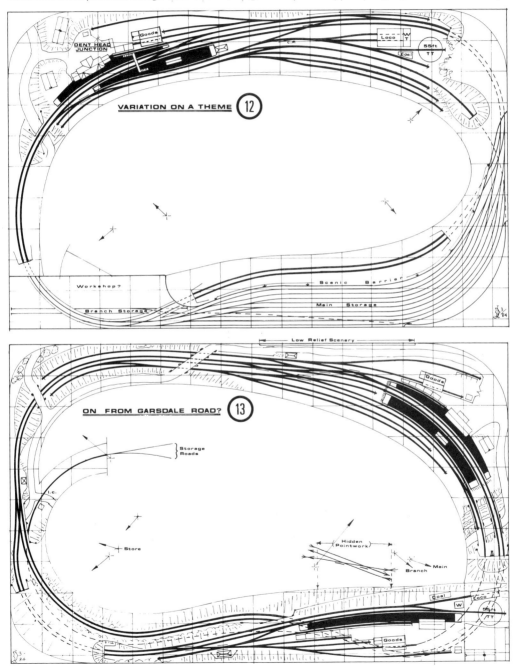

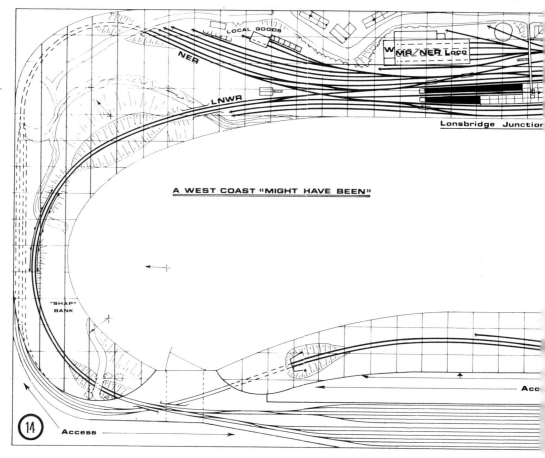

consequence, be unnecessary to have the terminus capacity matching that of the storage roads.

The continuous link in front of the terminus approach tracks is, as in many of my more recent schemes, largely 'window dressing' for testing and 'tail-chasing' purposes. The idea is vaguely similar to my first Kendal scheme but, had I built it, I think I might have re-written the story line in order to try and make the main station a Midland/LNWR joint affair with the terminus belonging to the company which operated the main line. This sort of story seems to have quite a lot of scope for the modeller who fancies two companies but does not want them equally represented.

Fig 14 *A West Coast 'might have been'* Every now and again one hears of a modeller who has the sort of space in which he or she can create the stuff of which dreams are made. This plan is to meet the needs of just such a person but lest the reader should dismiss it as simply a wild fantasy, born out of an over-imaginative mind, let me state from the outset that this layout is actually being built, moreover in 7 mm scale at that! Interestingly, when I gridded the drawing with the usual 4 mm scale 12 in squares, I found it was not much bigger than my final 4 mm effort (Fig 3). What we cannot figure out is how long it will take to finish it, but I have seen trains circulating on one of the main lines already.

The requirement was a difficult one — an 'Edwardian' period pre-group system, somewhat similar to that of the late W. S. Norris, with the Midland, LNWR and North Eastern strongly represented — along with some 'funny' trains out of sight, ranging from SE&CR boat trains to 14 teak coaches headed by a Gresley 'Pacific'. As an LMS enthusiast I was tempted to comment that one couldn't get much 'funnier' than that! At the same time, my friend did not wish for the 'model museum' approach adopted by Mr Norris in somewhat similar space circumstances. The layout had to look prototypically feasible both in appearance *and* operational terms even though for much of the time the main requirement would be to see trains simply running in a setting which made sense. Moreover, given the size of the site it was possible to envisage an infinite number of layout types. Indeed, one of the real problems of a big site is that there are so many perfectly reasonable ways of using it that it is often difficult to know where to start. Most of us have the solutions forced on us by the site restrictions — but not in this case.

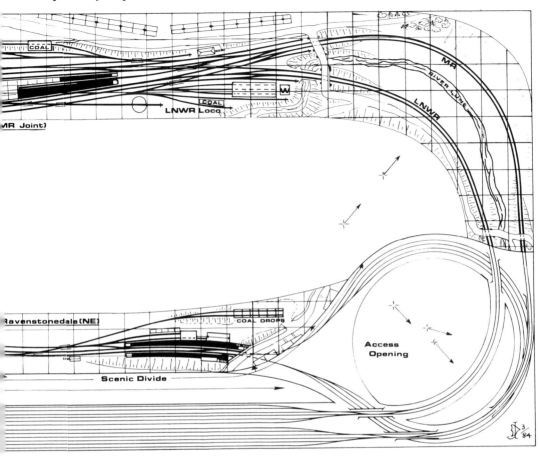

Eventually, I recall saying, in effect, 'Just supposing the Settle and Carlisle had never been built, what would Tebay have been like?' I chose Tebay because of the NER link and the net result was a rebuilt Tebay station ('Lonsbridge Junction') to accommodate the LNWR and MR traffic plus the existing NER trains. The real-life Low Gill Junction, a few miles to the south, is assumed to have been abandoned as too cramped for space and, in consequence, the Midland has felt obliged to build its own new line up the Lune valley on the opposite side to that of the LNWR. Moreover, we have also assumed that since it was the MR which wanted to get to Carlisle, the LNWR would have insisted that the Midland footed most of the bill for the rebuilding of Tebay. In consequence, much of the station layout and architecture would follow Midland practice.

The junction layout adopted is virtually that of Hellifield, modified to suit the double junction requirement at both ends. The NER passing station, which conceals the storage roads, will be based in visual terms on the very pretty North Eastern stations in the hilly areas of the North, including a set of typical coal drops. The 'funny' trains will live in the 'NER' loops but, otherwise, the layout can be operated in truly prototypical fashion. The main storage loops are long enough to take two trains each and thus allow end to end operation (ie, from one end of the loop via the junction to the other end of the loop — or the NER branch if desired). I used the same idea on the 'Little Long Drag' to good effect and it has the additional advantage of allowing display running of uni-directional 'tail-chasing' trains by a single operator.

Although a huge layout by conventional British standards, it is essentially both believable and simple in concept. The basic ideas could be put into a much smaller space if required — indeed Fig 13 is based on a not dissimilar theme. The influence of my 'Little Long Drag' (Fig 3) is not accidental and yet, in spite of all this space, I cannot resist commenting that even this layout has to compromise on curve radii, if very little else!

Chapter 5

Research

'Research: diligent and protracted seeking of facts or principles; laborious or continued search after truth; investigation; to search again; to examine anew.'

Dictionary definition

I sometimes think, when reading some of the letters sent to me and my friends, not to mention occasional pleas for information in the model magazines, that our correspondents may have read the dictionary definition of 'research' and decided that it is too hard or too boring to justify their own efforts and that they imagine that by some wave of a magic wand, the fruits of an individual's research can be made 100 per cent available for the price of a stamped addressed envelope — sometimes without the stamp!

The truth is far less simple and I often feel very concerned lest many modellers give up too easily. To be frank, I never know how to answer the letter which, in effect, says: 'Please let me have all the information you have gleaned about . . . over the last 20 years or so'. Virtually any objective reply would appear rude and inconsiderate so I feel it would be helpful if I tried to explain the business of research as I see it and, hopefully, encourage would-be historical modellers to have a go for themselves.

61

62

Plates 61 and 62 Research can be carried out at a variety of levels for a variety of purposes and is limited only by the individual's own inclinations. However, there is little doubt in my mind that photographs are essential for almost all lines of investigation and crucial to the modelmaker. The amount they can reveal depends on the input given by the investigator but in this chapter a fairly mixed bag of pictures is offered to try and demonstrate some of the ways pictures can be used, starting with the locomotives itself. The two pictures here show examples of the Midland Class '3' 4–4–0 passenger engine in Midland days and LMS days respectively. Most modellers at some time wish to know how particular favourite types looked at the time they seek to model and are aware of the fact that changes took place. At the most superficial level this may be no more than a change of livery — but how vital this one aspect can be in establishing authenticity.

In this pair of pictures there is obviously a difference in livery, as evidenced by the layout of the insignia. The Midland version (No 775) is red, the LMS version (No 767) lined black. This fact is not clear from the picture and demands pre-knowledge. However, detail changes can be determined if the picture is analysed systematically. It is best to start at the same end of the engine in both cases and work backwards, using a magnifying glass if need be.

Thus, it can be seen that the smokebox of No 767 is heavily rivetted and extends further forward than No 775. This is because No 767 is in superheated condition and this immediately suggests the need to find out when it changed shape in this important respect. The smokebox doors are not quite the same and the top lamp irons are in different places. Moving back along the engine it can be seen that the safety valves are in a housing on No 775 but open to inspection on No 767 — which also has a horizontal handrail below the cabside cut-away. The top pair of cab front windows are of different shapes — have a look carefully — and the tender of No 767 has a vertical centre beading whereas that of No 775 does not. Neither does it seem to have a bulkhead in front of the coal space. Looking again, the observer may also realise that No 767 has bogie brakes and visible inside cylinder tail-rod housings, while No 775 has splash plates in front of the bogie wheels.

All this and more from just one pair of pictures — and I have not yet got down to the two trains which are also interesting . . . the Lancashire and Yorkshire carriage behind No 775 for instance!

Clearly, there is insufficient space to analyse each and every picture in this chapter this way but I would recommend readers to do more than glance briefly at old pictures. They can reveal a great deal more that is not always even hinted at in the all too sparse captions in many railway books. In the pictures which follow, different uses of photographs will be considered (*D. Jenkinson collection, Real Photographs*).

Plate 63 This picture below was taken at Nottingham in April 1910 by the official MR photographer. It was taken to illustrate the handling of theatrical scenery but gives a welter of detail about many aspects of the Edwardian scene which would be admirably suited to a historical model of that period, even if this particular scene was not wanted. It is the kind of 'background data' picture which could be used by many modellers whether Midland inspired or not (*NRM*).

The point to bear in mind, first, last and always is that research is a means to an end in the context of historical modelling. The first task is to set some reasonable objectives of a tolerably practical nature and then do only such research as is necessary to turn these objectives into an end product. Of course, it is possible that, once started, the research element becomes of such absorbing interest that it extends well beyond the immediate requirements of the historical model itself — but this need not happen if the individual does not so wish. Fortunately many research workers (both modellers and non-modellers) have dug deeply into the archives and presented their findings in published books and articles — and I have found great personal pleasure and satisfaction in so doing, quite apart from my modelling interests. But I need not have done so, nor need anyone who wishes to make historical models. We cannot hope to get everything at second hand so I have tried to break down the subject into its main categories in order to simplify matters to some extent.

The importance of first hand knowledge and personal involvement

If a model railway is to satisfy, then it must be an individual creation. It can never be this if it merely copies, however well, the work of others. By all means take inspiration from fellow modellers but never slavishly copy them. Thus, the initial interest (however

Plates 64 and 65 Over the last few years, thanks to the ever growing number of interesting models offered by 'the trade' there has developed a wish to model prototypes from a period even before the modeller was born — and this includes many who chose the Big Four. These two pictures are included to show the LMS Railway at two very different periods in time because they seem to typify the scene at the period in question. This is not to say that the two trains could not have been seen at the same time but more to suggest that the overall character of the railway had changed.

The first view shows a pair of Class '5P4F' 2-6-0s — more familiarly nicknamed 'Crabs' — at the head of a typical Highland district train c 1930. The train is the up 'Royal Highlander' near Dunkeld and can be seen whistling for Hermitage tunnel. The formation of carriages displays the random 'mix' of vehicles very typical of the period. Contrast this with the tidy train in Plate 65, taken in 1948 at Willesden. The train is wholly Stanier from engine buffer beam backwards, although even at this date, such a degree of tidiness was by no means universal. Study of a number of pictures like this can do more than thousands of words to help the modeller acquire a sort of instinctive 'feel' for what is appropriate for his chosen period in time (*Gavin Wilson collection, R. W. Beaton*).

65

triggered off) must, sooner or later, be reinforced by first hand knowledge and experience. Let me give a personal example to demonstrate.

On several occasions over the last 20 years or so I have received letters from individuals who 'want to model the Settle and Carlisle'. I am, not surprisingly, flattered that I may have fired their imagination — but I am worried when the letters come from two or three hundred miles distant; for the first requirement is to go and have a look for yourself. Nothing, repeat nothing, can substitute for a personal acquaintanceship with the chosen prototype. You have to get a 'feel' for the place, its character and atmosphere. I have visited those high fells so often that I feel I know them as friends. I have basked in the sun picking wild strawberries at Dent Head, I have seen steam engines turning on the famous stockaded turntable at Garsdale, I have run for shelter from a squall into the platelayers' huts, I have been showered by an over-enthusiastic fireman taking water too

carelessly at Garsdale troughs, I have been frozen to the marrow at Batty Moss in mid-January waiting for the right moment to take a picture of Ribblehead (the resulting picture, by the way, was one of my best) and I have camped near the line to the accompaniment of an endless procession of night-time freight trains. I have ridden the line both behind and on the foot plate of steam and diesel and personally visited every single station.

Sadly, this is no longer possible. As these words are written the line is yet again under threat of closure and this time, I fear, there may be no reprieve — would that I could feel more optimistic. But I have to concede that for the last 10–15 years it has not been the real Settle–Carlisle as envisaged by its creators or as I first knew it. Hundreds of cars cluttering up the road at Ais Gill and mile upon mile of exposed film devoted to a handful of steam excursions is not what this line was really about at all; and I never visit now on these occasions — although I some-

Plate 66 This sort of picture is very useful if one wants to infer a particular operating area of a railway but does not wish to be too precise as to location. The picture was taken at South Hampstead on the LNWR main line from Euston but the train itself would suggest this route even if the location could not be identified. It consists of a readily identifiable mixture of LNWR and LMS standard stock, all painted red, behind an LMS-built Compound 4–4–0 in the pre-1928 style of painting. One does not have to have read much about the early days of the LMS to realise that this must have been a highly characteristic form of train on what the LMS called its Western Division (*BR LMR*).

Plate 67 This is the sort of 'oddball' which occasionally can be of real value in giving the keen modeller that 'something different' which is nevertheless quite authentically based. The push-pull train was a favourite prototype for modelmakers, largely because it took up relatively little space. But such trains all too often had a sameness about them which can be a bit repetitive when seen on layout after layout. The two coaches at the nearer end are themselves an interesting alternative to the single trailer coach usually modelled — and they are both conversions from erstwhile locomotive hauled stock of ex-LNWR type — but the two vehicles to the rear are not quite what they might appear to be. At first glance they seem to be the opposite end of a push-pull train which had its engine in the middle — a not uncommon feature — but on closer examination they reveal themselves to be conventional locomotive hauled coaches — an LMS standard lavatory composite and an ex-LNWR brake third running brake van inwards! They could either have been temporary strengtheners or the LMS could simply have been using the opportunity to use the regular two-coach push-pull train as a means of working a couple of empty coaches. The picture was taken at Kenilworth in 1938 (*Gordon Coltas*).

times ride on the trains themselves, for the scenery never changes — it really is immortal, thank God. But, even without the former activity, it should still be visited if you wish to model it. Choose a day mid-week when there are no fairground distractions and go up there to be alone with your thoughts — and let imagination take over. This way you will make a positive start — and it is just as true of the Somerset and Dorset, the West Highland, the Waverley route or whatever other railway interests you. It is not as easy as it once was since so many desirable lines are closed; but all railways had a sense of 'place' and the places are still there. Seek them out, get immersed in them and, when enjoying your evening pint or glass of wine, tell yourself that 'this is research' — for it is!

At this point you can start the more mundane search for information — that all-essential knowledge of the prototype to which I have several times referred. You may be lucky or you may have to work hard, I cannot tell; but I venture to suggest that it will prove more rewarding and enjoyable than you ever imagined. So . . . where does one start?

References and source material

I am, by nature, somewhat lazy and can see no point in re-doing work which someone else has already tackled. Therefore the starting point must always be to 'read, mark, learn and inwardly digest' any published material you can lay your hands on. Your local public library ought to be able to produce references for you of the more important published works and you could do a lot worse than ask them to get hold of

Plates 68 and 69 These two pictures, taken at Knighton Junction, Leicester — probably on the same day — are typical of many pictures which are not too difficult to track down at model shows and the like. Every historical modeller should try and find a few like this for his chosen period and area because they can be turned to again and again to answer all manner of detail points. For example they show quite clearly the painting of the back of signal arms in later Midland days, they give good detail of the engines concerned, both in detail terms and in respect of livery and they give quite a good indication of train formation — for example, the first five carriages in the passenger train are all different types and mostly of different style too on closer examination (*NRM*).

George Ottley's *Bibliography of Railway History* if you really want to see the 'Bible' of published railway literature.

Armed with a bit of information as to what has been written you can try and find it for yourself. Once again the public library could help — or, as is more likely, you may feel that you would like your own books, permanently. Write to the publishers for their lists (many, like Patrick Stephens Ltd, will send them free on a regular basis), read the small advertisement sections of the railway journals to try and locate secondhand book dealers, write to any local magazines inviting their readers to offer any information they have. I well remember, many years ago, that a short letter to *Dalesman* magazine produced a welter of interesting information about the Settle and Carlisle which was of great personal value to me.

If you live close to your chosen prototype then the local County Record Offices may have suitable information and, on a national scale, the railway archives at the Public Record Office, Kew, the Scottish Record Office in Edinburgh or, to a more limited extent, the library of the National Railway Museum, York, may be able to help; but be as precise as you can in making requests of these public bodies. It simplifies the task of searching for the material required and saves much waste of time when you get there. All these bodies operate on a 'prior appointment' basis and prefer dealing with specific requests rather than vague queries. The same is probably true of the County Record Offices as well.

A further fruitful source of accurate data is to be found in the various specialised railway societies. Some of them have 'open' membership (ie available to all who are willing to pay subscriptions); others are, in effect, 'closed' groups of active research workers. In the latter case (eg the LMS Society of which I am a founder member), the research output is either made available by published books and articles, readily available, or can be extracted by courtesy of a couple of stamped envelopes to the secretary, provided the request is couched in precise enough terms for the reply to be contained within the span of a single letter.

Back issues of model magazines and the journals of such organisations as the Historical Model Railway Society, the Stephenson Locomotive Society and the Railway Correspondence and Travel Society can also offer much of value. In the latter case, the RCTS Journal is a particularly valuable source of information on locomotive movements, duties and allocations.

Model Railway Exhibitions (usually advertised in the model press) can often be as valuable in drawing attention to special interest activities as for the more obvious displays of models and layouts which most go to see. Moreover, at these exhibitions, there are often displays by the protagonists of various different modelling scales which cut right across the company and period allegiances of the more specialised, company based, societies. It is here, too, that the potential historical modeller may find the best array of currently available literature or collections of historic photographs.

Where should the effort be directed?

There are numerous ways by which the research effort may be commenced. How far it is taken is very much up to the individual but, sooner or later, all research workers will encounter an area about which there is, apparently, no really useful published data at all and they are on their own. I am tempted to comment that this is the point which usually sorts out the men from the boys — but this would be unkind, since whether or not you wish to get into the realms of investigating basic source material has little or nothing to do with the desire to make or own models.

It is my experience, for what it is worth, that the most successful historical modellers are not always those with the most practical skill in model making, but are more often to be found in the ranks of those who are prepared to do that 'little bit extra' in the way of research and to make themselves knowledgeable (however reluctantly) in a few specific areas which are particularly relevant to their own field. Once again I will quote a personal example to make the point.

More years back than I care to recall(!) I realised that while most serious historical modellers of my acquaintanceship were very knowledgeable on such things as locomotive history and the detail variations thereof (and were quite keen on making freight stock and operating authentic goods trains), the passenger trains were not quite as I recalled them from my youth. This spurred me to investigate the passenger train more closely. In model terms it almost seemed that any appropriately coloured 'box' on a pair of bogies would suffice. This started off a line of

70

Plates 70 to 73 Sometimes it takes a series of pictures to reveal information which can be put to good use in model terms and I deliberately set out to find such a series, relevant to the Settle and Carlisle line, for this chapter. They all show the well known Edinburgh-St Pancras train heading south at various locations in the north country and span a period of just 20 years. They thus give virtually a potted history of one train during the whole of its LMS life.

The first picture, featuring Class '2' 4-4-0 No 470, was taken near Keighley in 1926. The train is composed mainly of ex-Midland clerestory stock plus three ex-NER six-wheel vans and is pulled by an ex-MR engine, rather giving the lie to those who regarded the Class '2' 4-4-0 as being too feeble for this kind of duty. The only LMS influence, other than the crest on the locomotive cabside, is the fourth passenger carrying vehicle — almost certainly one of the newly-built open third class coaches and being used for dining purposes.

By the time Plate 71 was taken (c 1938) the train had become 'The Thames-Forth Express' and is seen near Armathwaite behind LMS built Compound 4-4-0 No 1045 in the post-1928 standard red livery with lettering on the tender. The train is still only six coaches, of much the same generic type, and the ex-NER van traffic is still present. However, all the passenger coaches are now of LMS standard type, two each from the three identifiably different periods of LMS coach design.

The third view was taken at Ais Gill only a year later in 1939 and the presence of the 'Jubilee' 4-6-0 No 5568 *Western Australia* gives the whole ensemble a more modern look. The NER van is still there and the presence of the 4-6-0 suggests either that the train was running in strengthened formation, thus needing a bigger engine, or that for this particular job, anything between a Compound and a '5XP' would do, depending on availability. I am inclined to the latter view since for any train of any size at this time on this route, the LMS resorted to double heading to maintain the tight XL-limit timings of the late 1930s — see for example, Plate 56, believed to have been taken on the same day.

This view would be supported by the last picture (Plate 73) taken at Lunds viaduct in 1946 where the train, now eight coaches long, is in charge of a solitary Compound, No 1018. At this time, trains were running to drawn out schedules and there is no sign of a dining car, so the 4-4-0 would be quite adequate on its own. Note that the train is again all LMS stock but with a higher proportion of Stanier flush sided vehicles than the pre-war examples — and, at last, the ex-NER vans seem to have been pensioned off!

Now there is nothing in the above analysis which is beyond the capability of anyone who is willing to *examine* source material rather than merely look at it; but the information it can contribute to the accuracy of modelling is enormous. Obviously it demands a degree of pre-knowledge but this is not impossible to acquire (*W. Hubert Foster collection* — *NRM(2), M. W. Earley* — *courtesy NRM, E. E. Smith*).

71

72

73

research into LMS coaches, followed later by LNWR, WCJS, Midland, LYR etc, until, quite without realising it, I had become categorised, for want of a better phrase, as a 'carriage specialist'. It even spun off into my full-time work at the National Railway Museum wherein I have been extremely lucky to have been closely involved with our on-going restoration work on the historic carriages in the collection. This was not the original intention at all, although I am not complaining. I merely wanted to make more believable models! As an aside, it has had one rather practical benefit in that I now find myself making carriages for my friends in exchange for other items which I want but which they can make better than I can!

However, reverting to the main theme of the discussion, the amount and nature of research undertaken by the historical modeller will vary according to his specific needs, his personal inclination and the amount of information already available. There are no hard and fast rules but it may be useful to conclude this section by itemising those areas where, in my view, research will (or may) be necessary to provide the modeller with enough data on which to base his efforts:

a) The geographical, geological and human environmental characteristics of the area to be modelled, including buildings, landscape etc.

b) The specific distinguishing visual characteristics if any (eg, architecture/structures) of the chosen railway(s) — as opposed to the obvious matters of locomotive and rolling stock design and livery.

c) The individual operating peculiarities (as dictated by track layouts, loading facilities, passenger handling, disposition of buildings etc) of the chosen railway(s).

d) The appropriate locomotive class(es) for the period in question, their individual detail/livery variations and, if possible, the actual individual member(s) of the types associated with the chosen area or region.

e) The sort of traffic (passenger and freight) likely to be appropriate for the period/area chosen and the most logical railway response in terms of vehicle type, style, livery and quantity.

f) The correct (or near-correct) provisioning of such ancillary equipment (eg, platform 'furniture', road vehicles etc), as is needed to reinforce the overall picture and which is likely to increase 'believability'.

g) The authentic operating characteristics of the chosen railway at the period in question.

If one can accept that the above criteria are reasonably logical and all-embracing, then it should not be too difficult for the modeller to direct his research efforts into those areas which seem least well covered. This, at least, will reduce the likelihood of duplication of effort. It will not guarantee that all the required answers will be found but it should enable the modeller to make an informed guess as to the likely situation in those areas where hard evidence is lacking. To put it another way, I refuse to be diverted from modelling the Settle and Carlisle c 1930 simply because I do not know precisely how many cattle wagons were shipped from, say Lazonby or Appleby. My researches have given me sufficient data to be able to say 'It is likely that . . .' — and that for me is near enough for all practical purposes.

In the realm of historical research it was never more truly said that 'The best is the enemy of the good' and I feel truly sorry for those who fail to start their model making simply because they have been unable to cross the final 't' or dot the last 'i'. Most of them end up dead before they do anything!

Conclusions

Research is very much a matter of individual inclination. I do not believe that a successful historical model can be tackled without some research input but neither do I subscribe to the 'total perfectionist' approach. My views can be encapsulated in two main principles.

Firstly, while paying due regard to the published efforts of other researchers, I would state as a matter of principle that it is impossible to rely totally on the work of other people. No two railway historians have exactly the same outlook on the subject and it is crucial that there should be an individual and personal input, however modest, to the final synthesis for each and every modeller. I can only draw attention to areas which seem to me to be of relevance and interest but I cannot, nor would I wish to try to claim that any of my ideas should be regarded as anything more than 'thought inducing' stimuli.

Secondly, I would caution any potential historical modeller to be very careful to distinguish between the 'essential' and the 'amusing but irrelevant' information which his or her researches will unearth. Such byways will merely distract and, however

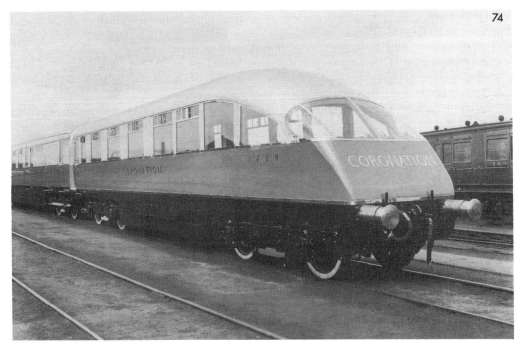

Plate 74 With the passage of time, pictures taken for one purpose are often of more value in quite a different context. This view is a very typical official record of a new type of carriage — in this case the celebrated 'beaver tail' observation cars of the LNER 'Coronation' train of 1937 — but what about that antique on the right? This is really much more interesting because it is an ex-LNWR 50 ft arc-roof corridor coach sold to the M&GN in 1935–6. It started life as LNWR No 1454, later 3649; then it became LMS 8339, later 4465. It is shown here as M&GN No 14 and then became LNER 83009 and later still 63327. Built in 1901 it was finally withdrawn in 1951 — and that is not all this picture can tell us. The carriage is still in fully lined out LMS livery and in good order too . . . and it is still gas lit. How many LNER modellers had realised they could run fully lined LMS liveries on their own company's vehicles I wonder! (*NRM*).

fascinating, contribute very little to the attainment of your ideal. On the other hand, there is no harm, *per se*, in allowing yourself to be distracted — provided that you are prepared to accept that some of your (possibly precious) time will be wasted on the acquisition of quite useless and irrelevant information!

This is the fascination of railways and the historical modelling thereof. There are no hard and fast rules and if you, the reader, feel that I have taken many thousands of words in this book to make this not very startling point, I can only apologise. What I have tried to do in this and the preceeding chapters is to analyse the situation as I see it and, as far as I am able, point out that there are no people with some sort of 'God given' solution to the many issues which may arise. Modelling, like painting or music or any other art form is, above all, a personal thing. I do not apolo-

gise for using the phrase 'art-form' because I truly believe that good modelling is an art, in every sense of the word. Who, when contemplating the work of such craftsmen as John Ahern, Peter Denny or my late friend Gavin Wilson, could possibly deny that in their craftsmanship is also to be found true artistry? The fact that they, I am sure, had no such thoughts in their mind makes it all the more meritorious. There is a sub-conscious element which is apparent to anyone who is prepared to let his (or her) imagination take full rein.

I could almost be tempted to conclude my efforts at this point; but since my brief was to produce a rounded exposition of historical railway modelling I feel I should try to encapsulate the whole business in some more detailed practical statements. This I have tried to do in the final chapters and appendices.

Chapter 6

The final synthesis

'The nice thing about the hobby is that we are our own general managers'

J. H. Russell

In the last analysis, the most important aspect of any historic model is that it truly satisfies the wishes of its creator. It matters not whether we please Mr X or annoy Mr Y. What is really important is that the end product should be as close as possible to that which we as individuals hold most dear. Since this is very much a personal issue, it is difficult to know the best way to bring the threads together, but I will try.

My original intention was to write the concluding chapters as a theoretical exercise in layout planning from site to final operational considerations but it seemed that it might be of more practical benefit if I was to consider a real rather than a mythical series of problems; so I have chosen to take my own latest layout site and work through the various factors which went into the final plan now in process of construction. The problems encountered cover most of the issues raised in earlier chapters but I will have to leave the reader to judge whether or not my solution is consistent with the ideas I have been expounding.

Background

I have listed, on page 38, those criteria which I want my model layouts to meet and also explained why, finally, I adopted 7 mm scale in 1976. I feel sure that, for me, this change of scale was correct but, having moved away from a spacious garden shed, I realised that I would be lucky if I could find a replacement site as generously proportioned at a price I could afford. However, I had no real choice and just hoped for the best. The final plan to which I had been working seemed to offer most of what I really wanted so the hope was that a new site would enable

me to repeat the essence of this design — even if the overall shape was slightly different.

Before detailed planning commenced certain basics were established in my mind — not least the 'story line' behind the layout itself. In this particular, I have remained pretty well consistent for more than 20 years. The Settle–Carlisle is a main line, with all that this implies, so if one cannot model a main line with some degree of fidelity then the line itself is not really a suitable prototype at all. I have tackled the main line concept twice in 4 mm scale but in 7 mm it seemed better to revert to the branch line theme since the scale length would, obviously, be smaller, regardless of site.

Other than the Hawes branch — not really a very exciting prospect in either visual or traffic terms — there was no branch off the Settle–Carlisle, so I took the well documented, albeit abortive, petition to the Midland by the villagers of Dentdale to build them a branch and did just that in my imagination. At first I assumed the line went to Sedbergh (which I re-christened Marthwaite) but more recently I have 'extended' the hypothetical line as far as Kendal to produce a sort of Midland Railway equivalent of the LNWR Windermere line. This involved a bit of consequential juggling with the real railway geography of the area — but nothing excessive — and the resultant revised railway network is shown in Fig 15. From this it will be seen that the terminus at Kendal is, in effect, Midland and Furness and that routes go to both the Midland main line at Dent Head and the Furness main line at Arnside. I have also imagined a triangle at Natland which comes into its own when

75

Plates 75 and 76 In establishing desirable criteria for a model layout it is normal to seek variety — if for no other reason than the fact that it can get quite boring to build endless repeats of the same thing. Once again, old pictures can come to our aid and these two views, both of trains associated with the Midland lines north of Leeds, give considerable scope for copying in model form. The first view shows a double headed train running under express headcode at Bell Busk c 1934. The choice of engines and stock makes me feel it must be some form of extra working. However, a 2–4–0 plus 0–6–0 combination of ex-MR motive power in front of a train consisting of a cattle wagon, five assorted ex-LNWR or LMS standard corridors and a couple of vans seems just the sort of thing to appeal to modellers.

The second picture, taken in the Bingley area at about the same time, shows much the same sort of bizarre combination of items on a stopping passenger train. This time it is an ex-MR 4–4–0 plus 0–4–4T combination and the train seems to contain four ex-MR clerestories, three LMS standard non-corridors (at the rear), an LNWR corridor leading and an unidentified short van in the middle. The latter seems to have distinct Glasgow and South Western lines. Even a part of this train would make an interesting model combination (*W. Hubert Foster collection — courtesy NRM*).

76

77

Plate 77 Few people have room for full-blown main line layouts yet there can be equally few who do not wish to own one or two proper express locomotives. The usual compromise is to run them in front of four or five corridors which, although it happened, was not very common. This picture, however, taken at Preston c 1937–38, indicates that from time to time, even the most glamorous engines could be found on local trains. The engine is 'Royal Scot' 4–6–0 No 6162 *Queen's Westminster Rifleman* and the train is made up of two three-coach local sets of mixed LMS standard and LNWR parentage. I have no doubt that from time to time, the train may well have been shorter and it does seem to me that if one is forced to limit train lengths to three or four carriages, there may well be some point in making them of this kind, rather than pretending that they represent a main line crack express (*Eric Treacy — courtesy P.B. Whitehouse*).

devising the operating sequence. When built, the terminus at Kendal will be predominantly Midland in character since it is assumed that the Midland would almost certainly have been the instigator and the Furness would probably have settled for 'running powers' rather than joint ownership.

So much for the story line — which can be developed ad infinitum with a knowledge of the local geography to help in assessing traffic potential. Next to establish was period. In order to give a Furness element to the finished model I felt I ought to go for a period before the FR engines had been

mostly scrapped. I have a preference also for the fully lined LMS period of livery. Full lining was suppressed on carriages from c 1934 onwards and only a handful of engines were painted red after 1927 so I thought that 1928–30 seemed about right and, as far as the main model collection is concerned this will be the 'target' period. Thus, the latest locomotive I would be prepared to operate in what I call the 'purist' mode would be a prototype built no later than 1930; while the liveries adopted would be a mixture of pre-28 and post-27 styles to suggest the time of changeover. Thus, for example, the first two

'Baby Scots' ('Patriots' in later days) were running-in brand new from Leeds in 1930, so if I modelled say, *Sir Frank Ree* as built, without smoke deflectors, this would nicely date the layout.

Of course, I could have opted for a purely pre-1923 display but this would have denied me the chance to have some of the very attractive carriages built by the LMS during the wood-panelled period (1923–30); so the date more or less chose itself. The little Furness 'Sharp-Stewart' 4–4–0s, of which I have a fine model, were actually scrapped a bit before 1930 but I am assuming that one was kept going for a year or two longer to operate the Kendal–Barrow trains! After all, who is to say precisely what subtle differences there might have been in history had the LMS inherited a network such as I have envisaged? That is the beauty of the 'just supposing' principle.

This, then, was the background against which I wanted to design a new layout. Typically, trains would be quite short (both passenger and freight) but a real line 24 miles long would develop some main line characteristics (as did the Windermere branch) so it seemed not unreasonable to assume a fair amount of mineral traffic and at least one or two through passenger workings to London (or at least Leeds) in the summer — again analagous to the Lakes Express on the Windermere line. While this sort of thinking is more properly part of the timetable and operational side of the story, it is rather important to have the basic outline in mind in order to plan the layout properly. Real railways were built to fulfil real needs and for a model to convince, it should look capable of handling the sort of traffic which is offered. Facilities should not be too lavish (this would not get past the shareholders on the grounds of expense), nor should they be inadequate (traffic would be lost or delayed, thus reducing revenue). Consequently, the detailed design of the track plan should be undertaken against the known (or likely) traffic to be handled. I shall return to this theme later, but firstly it is necessary to see whether the site available gives any prospect at all of accommodating the type of layout required. If not, then it is back to the thinking stage again.

Site considerations and the layout plan

When I bought my new house, the only really possible site (short of stealing a pair of attic bedrooms!) was a series of interlinked cellars below the whole property. It was, by a long way, the most awkward shape I had ever encountered but, from every other domestic point of view, the move made sense. There was obviously room to put *something* in the cellars but it was going to be a bit of a novelty to decide what. The site plan is given in Fig 16 and, to complete the picture, I should mention that the garden site is a sloping one, which makes floor level in the cellars approximately the same as the garden outside. I thus had an option of going outside if this seemed helpful. There was only one possible point at which the wall could be broached for this option and this too is marked on the plan, along with the three main cellars, A, B and C.

At first I began to regret abandoning 4 mm scale because quite an amusing system could have been envisaged but it would have been somewhat complex and I had by now become totally won over to the rolling and performance characteristics of Gauge '0' so I resolved to have a go. Cellar 'A' looked a possibility for a terminus but was really far too narrow to allow adequate development and still give access so it seemed to me inevitable that its rôle could only be that of hidden storage. This left the main cellar 'B' and the smaller cellar 'C' with its semi-circular end. The shape of the latter suggested a reversing loop but the diameter ruled it out in 7 mm scale. All that could go into 'C' would be another single-ended feature. Could this perhaps be the terminus site?

The main cellar offered an unrestricted 19 ft × 13 ft area, just sufficient to get in a continuous circuit off which I might throw spurs to the storage and terminus areas. This produced a sketched scheme (Fig 17a); but this was immediately thrown out because it did not permit end-to-end operation. As can be seen, both terminus and the storage lines would join the circuit in the same orientation so end-to-end operation was not possible.

The next problem, therefore, was to throw-off the junction to the terminus (or the storage roads) in opposite directions and thus allow end-to-end running (Dent Head to Kendal if you like). A scheme was devised (Fig 17b) which seemed possible and this was developed in some detail (Fig 18), after quite a number of false starts I might add. But I was not happy about the nature of the continuous circuit. It seemed a bit pokey and unrealistic, yet I did want a continuous facility. Not only do I like to indulge in 'tail-

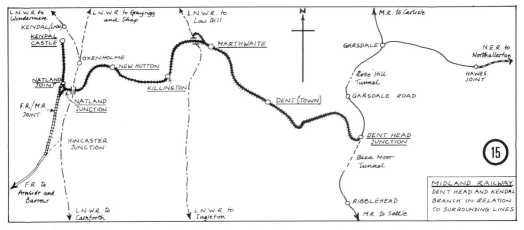

Fig 15 This map, not to precise scale, shows how the railway network of the north west Pennines would have looked, given the story line postulated by the author.

Fig 16 Site plan of the space available (1982 onwards) for the current layout proposals.

Fig 17 (a) and **(b)** These two sketches show, clearly, the convolutions necessary to obtain end to end operation in this awkward site. The upper drawing obviously does not solve the problem and, in order to get both reasonable radii and gradients, the complexities of the lower scheme are needed.

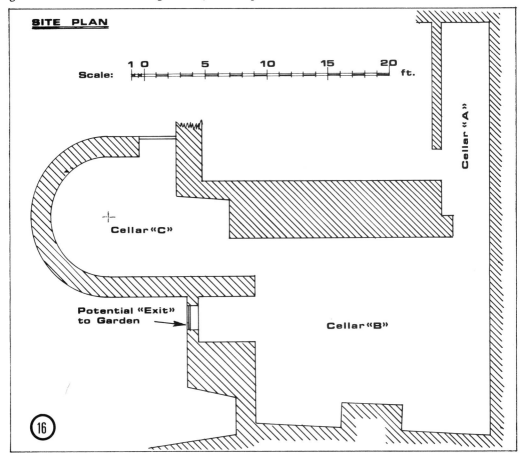

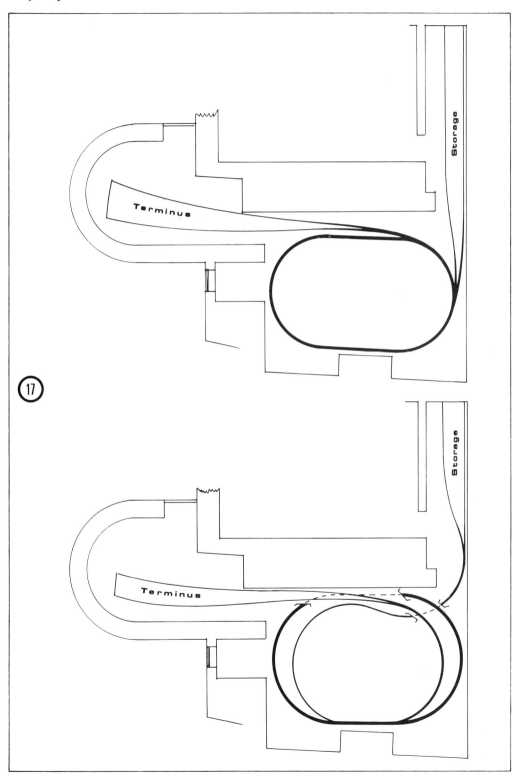

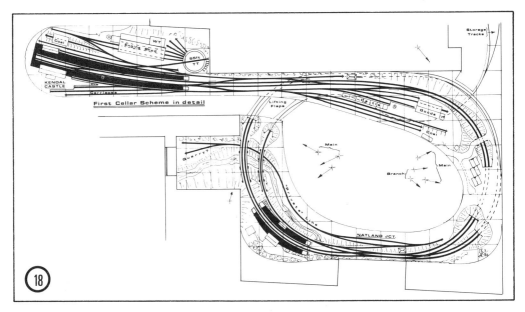

Fig 18 *First Cellar scheme in detail* This detailed scheme shows how Fig 17(b) was developed in 7 mm scale, although the grid squares scale the usual 12 in for 4 mm scale consistent with the other plans. The principal objections perceived by the author are the somewhat cramped and unconvincing nature of the continuous circuit (barely more than a simple circle of track), the rather unsatisfactory form of the station at Natland Junction and the number and magnitude of the gradients involved. Nevertheless, given limitations on train lengths it would have been operationally feasible and the terminus layout at 'Kendal' is one of the better solutions I have devised. This would have been a very interesting proposition in the same physical space in a smaller scale utilising similar track layouts and almost persuaded me to revert to the 4 mm scale format. In this scale, both the continuous circuit and the station at the junction could have been developed more realistically with consequent improvement in appearance.

Fig 19 This revised sketch scheme, now incorporating the 'outside' option, offers considerable improvement in scope compared with Figures 17(b) and 18, not least in the realm of length of main line run.

Fig 20 *Cellar scheme Number 2* This detailed working up of Fig 19 includes only such details as differ from Fig 18, the terminus being presumed the same. In this plan, Natland has developed slightly more believable characteristics but the single line cut-off from the terminus to the storage area which forms a sort of boundary to the whole system, would involve even more fearsome gradients than Fig 18, not to mention a multiplicity of places where tracks cross over each other. For this reason, the scheme was abondoned, although without this cut-off, it had some points in its favour.

chasing' from time to time, in spite of my earlier comments about its overall unsatisfactory nature, but in my experience it is the best possible way of 'running-in' motors in particular and stock in general.

The outside option was beginning to suggest itself more and more and when I saw Ken Paynes' '0' Gauge layout (*Railway Modeller*, July 1981) I realised that I could use his idea in my cellar. It's always sound policy to copy an individual good idea, even though I knew that my site was quite dissimilar in other aspects. Thus the next sketch scheme (Fig 19) emerged and this seemed to have real possibilities. The main problem seemed to be winter operation when I might

not wish to go outside. Was it possible, I wondered, to incorporate some way of getting from the terminus to the storage area *without* traversing the garden? I was prepared to sacrifice continuous operation for part of the year if I could at least operate end-to-end during the cold weather. I thus worked out a modification and again developed it in some detail (Fig 20). This one stayed on the drawing board for six months or more while I went on building carriages! But, eventually, I concluded I did not really like it. There were too many awkward gradients, too many locations where tracks passed one over the other and too many awkward duck-unders and the like. And, by

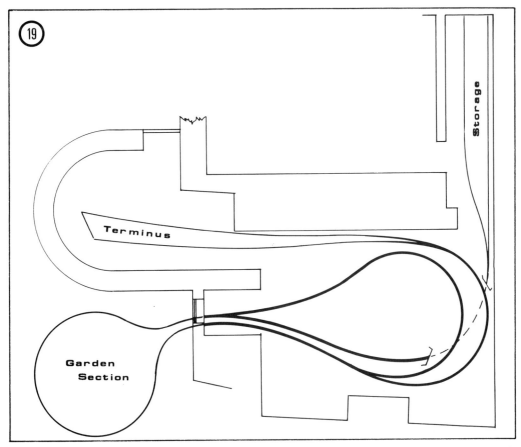

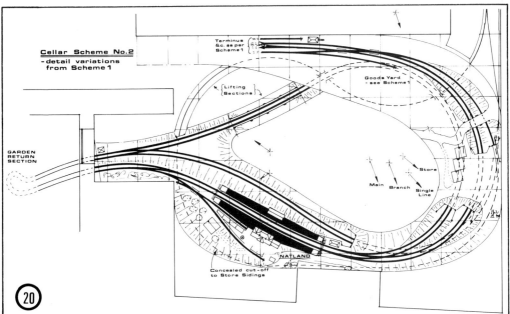

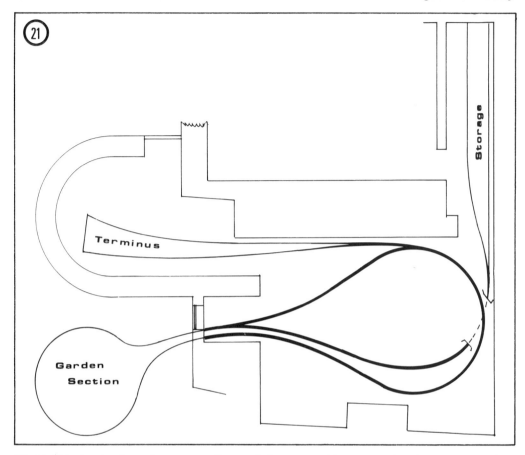

Fig 21 This sketch scheme is, conceptually, much the same as Fig 19, save that the junction has been moved to the other side of the site and, in consequence, shortened the length available for the terminus.

now, the junction had also sprouted a small station which, on reflection, seemed a bit too tiny.

The main reason for all these problems was my wish to have a good lengthy terminus at Kendal — it was likely to be the only real station — so I had tended to place the junction alongside the chimney breast and had to arrange matters so that the main line passed below the terminus approaches. It then occurred to me that if I moved the junction round the corner most of my problems were over — and a new sketch scheme emerged (Fig 21). I still could not get from terminus to storage without traversing the garden but maybe this would not be as irksome as I had feared. The problem then became whether I could model a reasonable terminus in the reduced length available. A few preliminary scribbles made it seem possible provided I

accepted some limitations in the facilities at the terminus.

At this point, therefore, I tried to work out in detail the minimum facilities needed at the terminus. Just how many platforms would be needed and how long should they be? In effect the fewer and shorter they were, the better it would be. The same also applied to freight and locomotive facilities. But the overall benefit seemed worth struggling for. Moreover, by moving the junction to its new position, I could perhaps contemplate developing the long reverse curve along the opposite wall as a genuine through station.

It remained to determine whether, within the spaces now defined, I could plan track formations which could handle the traffic, which looked rational and which the Midland might have adopted. There was nothing I could do to avoid the many long curves, save to make them as big as possible and hope that I could so organise the scenic developments as to minimise the visual problems. Thus, the final developed scheme was drawn up (Fig 22). I found that there was only one short stretch of main line (mostly in a tunnel) where I would need to go below 6 ft radius (5 ft 3 in actually) and that, in spite of the curvature, it was possible to design quite an effective through station which could also function as a temporary terminus in winter (should I not wish to use the outdoor area) thus allowing the system to work out and back from Kendal.

The biggest detail problem was the terminus layout itself. Terminus design has its own unique problems and I have never found it easy to design terminal stations. My first EM Gauge effort (Marthwaite) was a terminus and it went through two major rebuilds before I got it close to my liking. The embryonic Kendal was even worse. The difficulty was that which may well have faced the real railway builders — how to get all required traffic facilities into a restricted urban space. Those readers who remember Leeds Central station (ex-GNR/LNER) will remember what a cramped place it was and how short its platforms were for the important trains which used it — and Kendal (Castle) has, in the event, turned out to be rather similar.

The stumbling block was carriage sidings. My envisaged operational pattern involved the need to 'park' at least two sets of coaches from time to time and no matter how I tried, I could not find adequate space. Then one night, travelling back by train through the modern Leeds station (formerly Leeds City). I noticed the track arrangement between Platforms 2 and 3 (the old LNWR bit for those with a sense of history). Two quite short carriage roads are crammed in at the terminal end *between* the two platform roads but all four converge to two tracks by the time the platform end is reached. In 1984, these bays are served solely by 2, 3 or 4-car DMUs but I reckon a 3/4 coach local passenger set would not take up any more room. At all events, I finally got a track plan for the terminus which I quite liked and, for those interested, Fig 23 shows just a few of the many discarded attempts along the way. The final choice is developed from the last plan in the series, but it may well change again before tracklaying is completed.

Operational needs and layout planning

I inferred earlier that the final detailed design of track plan should relate to two considerations — site constraints and desired operational and traffic patterns. In practice these two will probably proceed in parallel but I have chosen to separate them for analysis and we must now consider the question of operation. I am going to deal with this problem solely in the context of the model which is designed to be operated in a semi-purist mode. After all, there is no reason to waste valuable time on planning 'operationally feasible' track plans if all that is wanted is a simple display circuit on which to operate a series of favourite trains. In fact, one of the most effective layouts I have ever seen is nothing more than a plain double track oval round a garden in Gauge 1 fed by a single ended 'ladder' track of stored trains. The owner is a 'live steam' devotee and I can personally vouch for the sheer delight in sitting on the lawn, glasses in hand, with a pair of live steamers circling in opposite directions for half an hour or more on 'one fill' as it were. However, not for the first time, I digress somewhat!

The essential point to remember about good model railway operation is that it should mirror reality as far as possible. Real railways are, above all, economic arteries. Trains are not operated just because they look nice or because it is 'a long time since the last one'. Consequently the first and overriding need is that the pattern of traffic should make sense in relation to the geographical and economic characteristics of the area modelled, real or imaginary. Given that this can be established, then it is logical to suppose that we can select the appropriate mix of stock and prime movers to create the right impression. In other words we should *not* start by picking engines, carriages or what have you and then tailor the traffic to suit. Rather, we should devise the traffic pattern and discover what we really need to have. This is how the real railways did it and in model terms it can save immense amounts of time and money if we do not build or buy that which we do not need. Of course, this 'hard-line' approach may well exclude our personal favourites from consideration and this is why I (and many others) adopt the semi-purist line with a few favourites hidden from sight. So, to sum up the requirements, what we need to work on are the following:

a) The type of traffic pattern, passenger

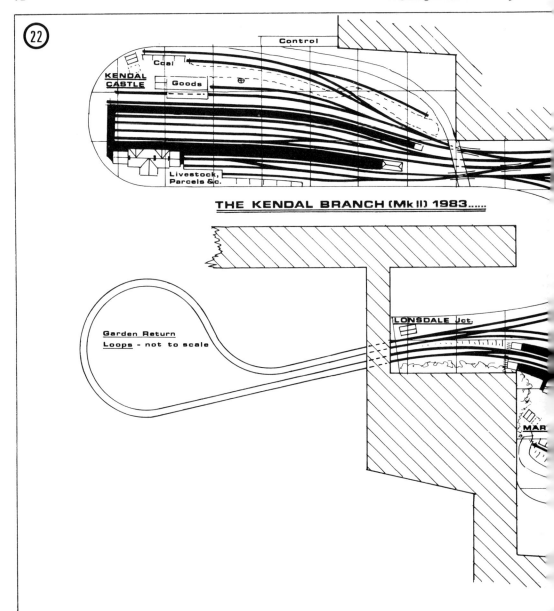

Fig 22 *The Kendal Branch (Mk II)* This scheme is the one actually under construction (1983 onwards) and although it may seem, superficially, just as complex as Figs 18 and 20, it is, in reality, much simpler — largely because of the easier gradients involved and the considerable reduction in the number of places where the tracks cross over each other. This latter feature cannot be wholly avoided but in this plan it has, at least, been kept to one location only.

Comparison with Fig 4 (its predecessor) will reveal that the concept is identical. The only real difference is that the former concealed double junction (Fig 4) has now become very visible and named 'Lonsdale'.

The detailed design of both 'Kendal' and 'Marthwaite' was not easy and I cannot guarantee that they will emerge in precisely the same detail as drawn. Some of the preliminary ideas for 'Kendal' are given in Fig 23 but 'Marthwaite' had but one earlier discarded plan. This would have placed the platform at the tunnel end of the site and the yard was drawn out on the familiar Lazonby style. It neither suited the

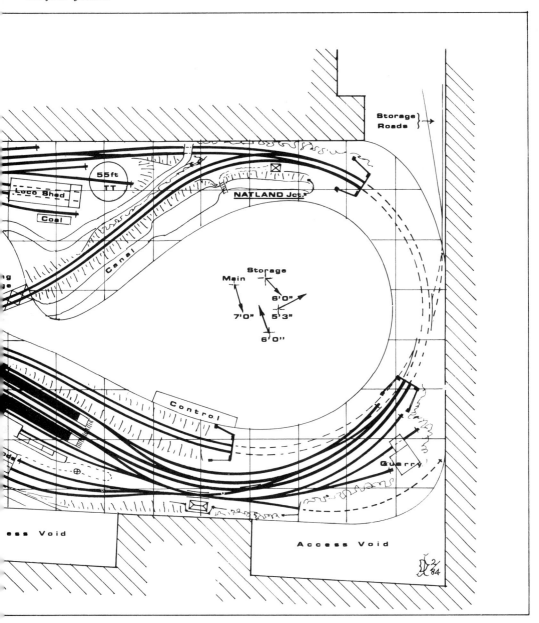

reverse curve nor the width of the site so I had to settle for the much revised version as shown. It is no longer a typical Settle-Carlisle through station but, interestingly and quite subconsciously, it has turned out to be very similar, schematically, to the very first 'Marthwaite' idea (Fig 1). Even the single line link to the 'LNWR' (hidden behind the quarry) is in much the same orientation as the old Haygarth branch and will carry much the same sort of traffic — so maybe predestination is not dead!

Of the many layout schemes I have planned, some included in this book, I do not consider this to be the best — merely the one which seems most likely to satisfy my present personal constraints in the most satisfactory way. I am not totally happy about the curve radius at 'Marthwaite' (7 ft minimum — 4 ft in 4 mm scale) and it is certain that a plan such as this would be inconceivable with commercially available pointwork; but it has begun to take on some character already and if I can get it working reliably, it could well be the most operationally satisfying layout I have ever built. As usual, the grid squares represent 12 in in 4 mm scale although the marked *dimensions* are for my 7 mm project.

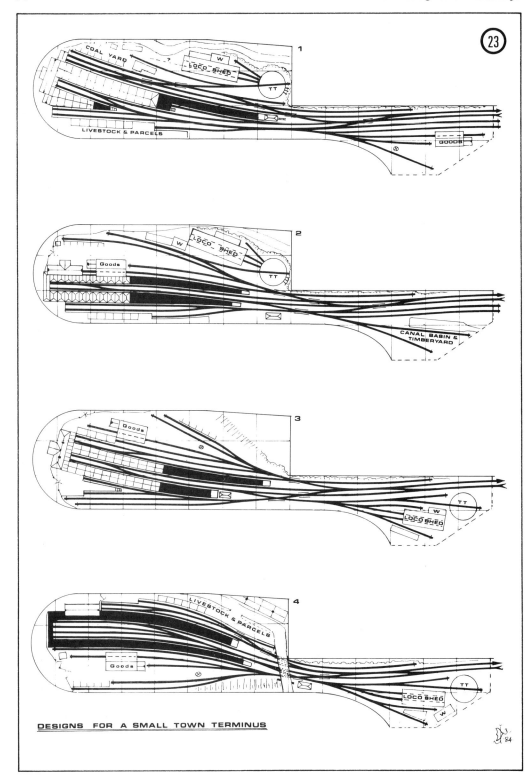

1

COAL YARD
?
W
LOCO SHED
TT
LIVESTOCK & PARCELS
GOODS

2

W
LOCO SHED
Goods
TT
CANAL BASIN &
TIMBERYARD

3

Goods
W
TT
LOCO SHED

4

LIVESTOCK & PARCELS
Goods
TT
LOCO SHED
W

DESIGNS FOR A SMALL TOWN TERMINUS

Plate 78 Although the real railways had more space available than most modellers they were not always able to encroach far from their tracks and this picture demonstrates such a situation at Chester where there is almost no clearance between the main line and the vertical cutting wall. This sort of scene would, to my way of thinking, be a far more acceptable idea to copy where the model is close to a wall than to paint an open scenic background — even the tunnel seems placed for the modeller's benefit. The train is a Holyhead-Manchester express headed by rebuilt 'Royal Scot' No 46148 *The Manchester Regiment* and 'Britannia' 4–6–2 No 70046 *Anzac (Jim Carter)*.

Fig 23 *Designs for a small town terminus* These four drawings show some of the discarded ideas on the way to the scheme adopted at Fig 22. The final choice is clearly a modification of scheme No 4; but since this will be the last part of the layout to be built, it is at least possible that I may well revert to one or other of the earlier ideas. They could all handle the traffic and I may well opt for the one which seems, on site, to offer the greatest visual and scenic potential. I have included them all here because I want to reinforce the view expressed elsewhere in the book that there is rarely one perfect solution to a problem and it may be that one or two readers may find, in these alternative plans, some ideas which will prove helpful in a quite different context to my own.

'*En passant*', as it were, it might be worth mentioning that as an extension of my main layout concept, I was also seeking to evolve a terminus design which could, without modification, be 'plugged' directly onto a storage magazine at the main line 'exit'. This would enable part of the layout, at least, to be built transportable and be capable of possible exhibition operation on the 'terminus to fiddle yard' theme. All these designs would permit this and, as a conclusion to my comments on this particular drawing, I must acknowledge the considerable debt to my two friends Arthur Whitehead and Don Rowland who, over the years, have sent me numerous ideas to 'bite' on. They may recognise some of their own thoughts in these plans.

and freight to be reproduced.

b) An appropriate 'timetable' (or at least a train movement sequence) which will meet the requirements of (a).

c) The least amount of station and running line provisioning which will permit (a) and (b) to be achieved.

d) (Associated with (c).) Servicing facilities (eg, loco sheds, carriage sidings, repair shops) if appropriate.

e) The appropriate locomotives, carriages, wagons and other items (eg, road vehicles) which would handle such traffic.

f) (As a corollary to (e).) The correct train formations.

g) The operational aspects (related, of course, to (b) — above).

Once again, I shall use my latest design to illustrate the ideas, rather than discuss matters in a theoretical vacuum.

79

Plates 79 and 80 Station sites can take up a lot of room on a model and most of us seek for a widening of the baseboard to provide a suitable setting for station building and yard. This pair of pictures shows that this is not always necessary. They show opposite sides of the main station building at Staveley on the ex-LNWR Windermere branch which was literally built onto the side of the embankment, thus presenting a single storey elevation on the platform side and a conventional appearance on the other. This arrangement seems to have considerable application in modelling terms (*D. Jenkinson*).

80

81

Plates 81 and 82 These two pictures are designed to complement the previous pair, this time in respect of freight traffic. As with passenger stations, so too with goods facilities, most of us try to provide a proper goods yard and seek the space so to do. Then we have the problem of integrating the railway with the town or village scenery. At Burneside, also on the Windermere branch, some of the goods lines simply went down the village street to serve a paper mill and an adaptation of this idea might serve to dispense with a goods yard altogether yet still provide both scenic potential and freight traffic (*D. Jenkinson*).

82

Basic traffic patterns

If you are modelling either a real station or an imaginary line based on a connection with a real railway then the best starting point for passenger trains is almost always the public timetable for the period in question. This immediately tells you what sort of trains (and how many) were operated. For freight traffic it is best to try and find a copy of the working freight timetable. This can involve a bit of research into libraries and other collections but the help it gives more than compensates for the possible difficulty in finding a copy in the first instance. Freight traffic patterns tended to be more static than passenger operations — although there were, of course, exceptions — so it is not absolutely essential to have the same year's timetable for both. A few years either side of the chosen period should not show great differences save in rare circumstances.

In my case, the model will represent a branch which makes connections with the Settle-Carlisle at Dent Head and with the Carnforth-Barrow line at Arnside. I therefore looked up the times at which the 'real' trains passed or stopped at these points, c 1930, confining attention mostly to stopping passenger trains and pick-up freight services. I argued that the bulk of branch services would be related to this type of train rather than to the expresses and through main line freight services. It would always be possible to add a few more exotic workings! This preliminary exercise suggested that some six to eight daily passenger services on each route would connect with most main line stopping trains. This would give about

15 or so basic passenger arrivals and a similar number of departures from Kendal. To this I added a daily (summer only) through service from and to St Pancras via Leeds and the possibility of one or two summer (Saturday only) excursions — say one from the industrial areas of Yorkshire and Lancashire (via Hellifield) and one from the North East via the Wensleydale branch. I also felt that some form of connecting services would be needed from Marthwaite (Sedbergh) to the LNWR Low Gill line — possibly a railmotor shuttle — and that a few overnight coaches to London from Kendal would not be out of the question.

On the freight side, a morning and afternoon pick-up on each route would serve adequately to provide the basic facility, supplemented by the odd cattle 'special' and, hopefully, fairly regular mineral workings from the various lineside quarries. In this connection, knowledge of the local 'geography' of the area to be modelled is invaluable. Most branch lines (and main lines for that matter) generated, in local freight terms, a fairly typical pattern of traffic. There would be regular deliveries of coal for the local merchant(s), general merchandise (usually via a goods shed) for the local traders and, commonly, spasmodic livestock traffic at certain seasons of the year. More specialised traffic (eg, timber, steel, quarry material etc), would depend on the nature of the local geography and economic activity and this is where there is abundant scope for injecting one's own views into the model and letting it develop some 'personality'. This then gives a basic service pattern to be attempted and at

Fig 24 This diagram is a more refined version of the original 'Marthwaite' scheme given in Fig 1. It should be self-explanatory but it is worth remarking that, where possible, the real railways tried to achieve an easing of gradients through the station sites in order to facilitate stopping and starting of trains. This I have attempted to replicate here.

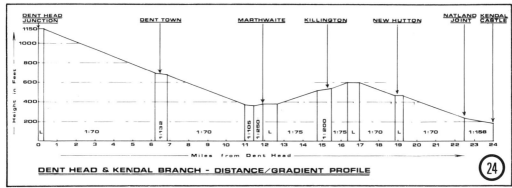

KENDAL CASTLE & ARNSIDE to MARTHWAITE & DENT HEAD — Monday to Saturday

								(SX)	(SO)	(SO)							(SO)				
KENDAL CASTLE	12a15	6b40		7 30		9 02	11 10		12d 32				2 20		4h15	4j 33	4 40			7b 10		10 30
Natland Joint	—	6 45		7 35		9 07	11 15		—				2 25		—	—	4 45			7 15		10 35
ARNSIDE			6 32		8 c 06			11 56		12e31	1f 40		3g 09					5k 05			7 56	
Sandside			6 38		8 c 12				12 02		12 37	1f 44	3g 14					5k 10			8 02	
Heversham			6 42		8 c 16				12 06		12 41	1f 48	3g 18	The Dalesman				5k 14			8 06	
Sedgewick			7 00		8 44				12 14		12 49	2 14	4 02					5 29			8 14	
New Hutton	—		6 54	7 05	7 44	8 49	9 16	11 25	12 19	—	12 54	2 19	2 34	4 07	—	—	4 54	5 34	7 25	8 19	10 44
Killington	—		7 02	7 12	7 52	8 57	9 24	11 32	12 26	—	1 02	2 27	2 42	4 15	—	—	5 02	5 42	7 32	8 27	10 52
MARTHWAITE	12a45		7 10	7 20	8 00	9 05	9 33	11 40	12 34	12d 54	1 10	2 35	2 50	4 23	4h37	4j 55	5 10	5 50	7 40	8 35	11 00
Dent Town	—		7 35	8 15		9 48	11 55	12 49	—	1 25		3 05	4 38	—	—	5 25	6 05	7 55	8 50	
DENT HEAD JUNCTION	1a10		7 55	8 34		10 08	12 14	1 09	1d 19	1 45		3 24	4 57	5h 03	5j 21	5 44	6 25	8 15	9 10	

a Through carriages and sleeping cars to London (St Pancras). Sleeping car passengers may join at Kendal from 10.30 pm.
b Steam Railmotor — third class only.
c Change at Sedgewick.
d To Leeds (Wellington); conveys through carriages to Bradford (Forster Square), Liverpool (Central) and Manchester (Victoria).
e From Barrow (dep 9.56 am).
f Change at Sedgewick, runs 10 minutes earlier (SO).
g Change at Sedgewick, runs 5 minutes later (SO).
h To London (St Pancras); dining cars conveyed throughout but meal service terminates at Derby. Through carriage(s) to Bristol (Temple Meads).
j To Newcastle (LNER); conveys through carriages for York and Middlesbrough.
k Runs 2 minutes earlier (SO) and change at Sedgewick (SO).

					(SO)	(SX)		(SO)				(SO)								
DENT HEAD JUNCTION	3a 50	7 45		9 00			10 25	10d 55	12 55	1 15	2e 35	2f 43		4 16	5 00		6 45	8k 30	9 10	10 20
Dent Town	—	7 55		9 10			10 35	—	1 05	1 25	—	—		4 26	5 10		6 55	8 40	9 20	10 30
MARTHWAITE	4a 10	8 05	8 10	9 25	9 45	10 05	10 45	11d 10	1 16	1 36	2e 50	2f 58	3g 16	4 36	5 20	6j 30	7 05	8 50	9 30	10 40
Killington	—	8 14	8 19	9 34	9 54	10 14	10 54	—	1 25	1 45	—	—	3g 25	4 45	5 29	6j 39	7 14	8 59	9 39	10 49
New Hutton	—	8 25	8 30	9 45	10 05	10 25	11 05	—	1 34	1 54	—	—	3g 36	4 56	5 40	6j 50	7 25	9 10	9 50	11 00
Sedgewick		8 29			10 09	10 29				1 58			3g 40	5 00			7 29		10 00	
Heversham		9b 14			10 17	10 37				2b 35	The Dalesman		4b 23	6h 07			7 37		10 08	
Sandside		9b 18			10 21	10 41				2b 39			4b 27	6h 11			7 41		10 14	
ARNSIDE		9b 24			10c 27	10 47				2b 44			4b 35	6h 16			7 47		10 18	
Natland Joint	—		8 36	9 50			11 11	—	1 41	—	—			5 46	6j 56		9 16		11 06
KENDAL CASTLE	4a 35		8 40	9 55			11 15	11d 32	1 45		3e 10	3f 20		5 50	7j 00		9 21		11 10

a Through carriages and sleeping cars from London (St Pancras). Sleeping car passengers may remain in their berths until 7.30 am. Sleeping car passengers for Marthwaite may travel to Kendal and remain in their berths until 6.30 am, returning at 6.40 am.
b Change at Sedgewick.
c To Barrow (arrive 11.20 am).
d From Leeds (Wellington); conveys through carriages from Bradford (Forster Square), Liverpool (Central) and Manchester (Victoria).
e From London (St Pancras); dining cars conveyed throughout, meal service commences at Derby. Through carriage(s) from Bristol (Temple Meads).
f From Newcastle (LNER); conveys through carriages from York and Middlesbrough.
g Runs 5 minutes later (SO).
h Change at Sedgewick and runs 4 minutes later (SO).
j Runs 2 minutes later (SO). Steam Railmotor — third class only.
k Steam Railmotor — third class only.

(25)

Fig 25 This, totally fictional timetable is really a piece of imaginative nonsense . . . but I enjoy the mental processes involved! I have also done one for the Kendal-Arnside and Marthwaite-Ingleton services. It is not, in fact, necessary actually to write out a timetable in this form in order to arrive at an appropriate operational sequence but, for those interested, the train graph at Fig 27 (Appendix I) starts, effectively, with the 9.55 am, arrival at Kendal from Dent Head. In accordance with good LMS practice, a vertical line between the hours and minutes columns denotes pm!

this stage it is possible to take stock and consider whether the modelling potential (suggested by the likely traffic patterns) is sufficient to sustain interest.

If so, the next stage is to evolve a sequence of train movements which will reproduce these features. In this chapter I shall confine myself to the principles involved but in Appendix I, I have gone into more detail of the mechanics involved in actually preparing the finished sequence in detail.

Train movement sequence

The first requirement is to assess how long it would take a real train of the type envisaged to traverse the full length of the route in real time and distance terms. Study of old time-tables will give some idea of elapsed time (related to distance) and this must then be modified, if necessary, to allow for favour-able or adverse gradients. Thus, for ex-ample, on my mythical branch line (gradient and distance profile, Fig 24) I reckoned it would take stopping passenger trains some 65 minutes to go from Kendal to Dent Head and some 10 minutes less in the opposite direction. Expresses stopping only at Marthwaite would be quicker; while pick-up freight trains would not only take longer than either between stations but would also spend some time at each station to shunt the traffic.

From this one goes on to establish a 'pub-lic' passenger timetable for the route, ideally in association with a train graph (see Appen-dix I) and this must be taken to completion — in other words it must include all possible passenger trains, including those which only run on certain days, eg, Saturdays in sum-mer. In my case this involved the three prin-cipal routes (Kendal–Dent Head, Kendal–Arnside (for Barrow) and Dent Head–Arnside (direct)), not to mention the addi-tional Marthwaite–Ingleton push-pull service. This was then translated to a quasi-official timetable part of which is given in Fig 25.

At this point, using the train graph, it is possible to find 'paths' (ie, periods of time between trains) wherein can be added the freight services (see Appendix I) and even-tually one can produce a complete sequence of train arrivals and departures (passenger and freight) at the terminal points, along with their passing times (or shunting periods) at the intermediate locations.

Track provisioning for traffic offered

It is now (at long last!) possible to consider more precisely the exact track provisioning which might be necessary. For example, if the timetable reveals that as many as three passenger trains will arrive at the terminus before any one of them subsequently de-parts, it may necessitate providing three separate platforms. Alternatively, it may be better to provide siding(s) into which stock can be shunted to make due allowance for programmed timetable moves. Only at this point can one really determine whether the proposed track layout is either too lavish or too limited for the traffic envisaged. In Fig 26 I have produced a 'track occupation' chart for Kendal Castle based on these principles. Study of this chart revealed that while, with some slight adjustments, two platforms might suffice, a third would be very desirable if possible. This would give a marginally surplus platform capacity for much of the time but would allow the insertion of 'extra' trains (excursions etc) without undue em-barrassment, not to mention the ability to use the extra platform as a temporary siding, goods arrival track or whatever.

Similar thought processes applied to the planned freight services and locomotive

Fig 26 Platform Occupation — Kendal Castle.

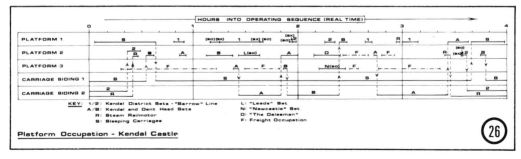

movements will also give a clear picture of how many sidings etc, (freight) or locomotive standing and servicing locations, in the loco shed area, will be needed; and from these one can then finally arrive at a coherent track plan for the terminus. The plan eventually arrived at in Fig 22 was worked out with these ideas in mind. A similar line of reasoning will also reveal the maximum occupation of any hidden storage sidings which may be incorporated. Obviously there should be enough separate tracks for each train or, if two trains must occupy the same storage road (for reasons of baseboard width) one must consider whether the siding is long enough to accept both trains and that the order in which the trains leave the storage is in 'reverse' of the way they entered . . . if not, something must be done!

A more difficult problem is encountered with passing stations. Normally (on a typical British two track line) they would have two passenger platforms, a main station building (with offices) and some form, however rudimentary, of freight facilities. How much elaboration on this basic theme is provided is very difficult to assess. To be honest, even the Midland got it wrong on the Settle and Carlisle itself where some stations were over-provided with facilities. Thus on my new system, 'Marthwaite' (Fig 22) will be designed to handle the level of traffic of a typical Settle-Carlisle station of the Lazonby, Armathwaite, Kirkby Stephen degree of activity. I have added a quarry loading facility (somewhat loosely based on that which was formerly located at Long Marton) and also assumed a rudimentary 'junction' with the single line link to the ex-LNWR line at the real location of Sedbergh. Only time will tell whether I have 'over-egged the pudding'. If so, I might indulge in a degree of track lifting and simplification.

A quite likely situation at this stage will be that there is either insufficient space to produce trackage for the desired operating pattern or, alternatively, that the optimum operating pattern is too restricted to justify the type of track envisaged or desired. It will be rare if you get it right the first time! On balance it is better if it turns out that the envisaged layout is too complex for the traffic on offer. It is easier to simplify the track layouts and this has, as a bonus, the visual effect of enhancing the spaciousness of the scene. If, however, the traffic pattern seems likely to swamp the layout facilities (this actually happened with my original 'Marthwaite' scheme of 1966-7) then a real problem is encountered. The best solution is probably to simplify the traffic pattern rather than make the layout excessively cluttered but, before starting to spend real money on building the wretched thing, it is necessary to arrive at a balance. Once this is achieved, we can look at the trains themselves.

Locomotive and rolling stock provisioning

With any luck all the above-mentioned theoretical planning should (or may well) have begun to establish, in the modeller's mind, a sort of 'character' which the finished model will, hopefully, display; for it is not as academic and sterile as it may seem. In fact, during one of many such sessions, it occurred to me that if I was not careful, I would have the set-up so well worked out in my mind that there may, perhaps, be no real need to actually build any models at all! Perhaps all I needed was a good track plan, a multitude of coloured pins to represent the trains, locomotives and so forth and a vivid imagination! Seriously, however, the next stage is to translate the pattern of traffic into trains, locomotives etc, and this is where the real fun begins.

First and foremost is an appreciation of the type of train(s) which will, most accurately, reproduce the workings required and the first essential is to establish 'how many?' I have analysed this process in detail in Appendix II so at this stage it is merely necessary to state that, in passenger train terms, the requirement turned out to be as follows:

a) For the Kendal–Dent Head service — two local non-corridor sets.

b) For the Kendal–Arnside (Barrow) service — two local non-corridor sets.

c) For the railmotor service — one push-pull driving trailer.

d) For the overnight service — between two and four through carriages.

e) For the principal London service — one main line corridor set, with five to seven vehicles.

f) For the 'Saturday only' excursion(s) — one or two sets of assorted vehicles.

— Plus, possibly, one or two spare vehicles.

It will be noted that the direct Dent Head–Arnside service (see Fig 15) is not covered.

83

84

This is because I realised that a crafty man-oeuvre was possible. Trains leaving Kendal for Dent Head would pass through Marth-waite in natural sequence and retain their identity. Trains from Kendal to Arnside would, on their way to the storage tracks, also inevitably pass through Marthwaite, which was a prototypical absurdity. But if, between Kendal and Marthwaite, they could somehow 'change identity,' they could be treated at Marthwaite as though they had not come from Kendal at all, but had originated from the Arnside line. The hypothetical tri-angular junction at Natland (Fig 15) would give geographical validity to this idea. All that was necessary was to insert a tunnel somewhere between Kendal and Marth-waite, where trains could be hidden so as to add verisimilitude to this deception. This is why there is a tunnel right at the Kendal end of Marthwaite station and the fact that it also conceals the sharpest radii on the layout (Fig 22) is by way of a bonus.

Thus it is that all trains (passenger or freight) leaving Kendal bound for the Barrow line (as I choose to refer to the Furness Railway section) will emerge from the tunnel at Marthwaite as though they had arrived from the Barrow direction. The only problem was whether the length of the tunnel could conceal trains of believable size. Close examination of numerous contemp-orary photographs from the late 1920s and early 1930s revealed that on by far the bulk of LMS local services in rural areas, trains were rarely more than four coaches long with quite

Plates 83 and 84 These two pictures exemplify the sort of trains which I hope will establish some of the 'what' and 'where' details of my new layout. The first view shows the prototype 'Patriot' — or, as I prefer to call it 'Baby Scot' — No 5971 in its original form without smoke deflectors. It only ran like this for a year or so — 1930–31 — and so would help date the layout. I would not have space for an express of this length but reckon I could accommodate six or seven coaches. Plate 84 actually taken at York around the time of group-ing, attempts to show the type of local train I feel would be suitable and the sort of engine it might have. It is a mixture of different types of Midland stock with an LNWR van at the front and would not have changed, appreciably, during the 1920s, save for the obvious matter of repainting in LMS colours and the odd carriage change. For a more rural line, it might be more appropriate to reduce its length by a vehicle or two (*D. Jenkinson collection*).

modest sized engines. Thus, I concluded that well thought out 'short' sets would not only be correct in prototype terms but would also help by taking up less actual layout space — either in tunnels or at station locations. This would, additionally, enable some dis-creet platform shortening and a few other slight adjustments to the general scheme to increase its apparent length.

Thus, I finally resolved the passenger train requirement, in detail, as follows:

1) Kendal–Dent Head set A; two coach LMS standard Inter-District Lavatory set (1927 build) plus, possibly one strengthener if needed and/or vans, horseboxes etc.

2) Kendal–Dent Head set B; Ex-Midland three-coach set of mixed types — exact nature as yet undetermined but probably two older thirds plus one newer composite of which at least one (probably two) will be brakes.

3) Kendal District set No 1; Ex-LYR 'LBL' three-coach set — assumed to have been 'cascaded' after grouping to less important services in replacement of with-drawn stock.

4) Kendal District set No 2; A 'scratch' assembly of pre-group stock up to four vehicles provided *none* exceed 50 ft. A mix of ex-LNWR and ex-FR would be appropriate.

5) Railmotor; Ex-LNWR 50 ft arc roof, third class only driving trailer.

6) Overnight carriages; one elderly (ex-MR, LNWR or WCJS) 12-wheel first class sleeping car; one LMS standard third class sleeping car (1928 stock); one corridor composite brake (pre-group). It is assumed that these carriages attach/detach at Dent Head to or from the overnight Settle–Carlisle main line trains.

7) Principal London service; five-coach basic corridor set plus, say, one through coach from an alternative destination. It would be mostly late pre-group or early LMS Standard stock — ie, a reasonably modern formation but not as up to date as, say, the principal services on the main line.

8) Excursion/Saturday only set; a motley collection of entirely pre-group stock of some age(!), mostly gangwayed and with a fair number of separate portions from different starting points — eg, Leeds, Bradford, Manchester and Liverpool.

To work all the trains, I reckoned I would need the following locomotives:

Kendal-Dent Head; two ex-MR 4-4-0 tenders, one of which could also work the 'overnight' coaches to Dent Head.

Kendal-Arnside (Barrow); two non-Midland types (to emphasise the different pre-group origin of this route). I have gone for an ex-LNWR 2-4-2T and an ex-FR 4-4-0.

Railmotor; ex-LNWR motor fitted 'coal' tank.

'London' service; Leeds based 4-6-0 or 4-4-0. In 1930 it would probably have been a small-boiled ex-LNWR Claughton 4-6-0 or Compound 4-4-0; but I shall, in due course, use one of the first two 'Baby Scot' 5XP 4-6-0s (built in 1930 and both, initially, sent to Leeds for a while) in order to date the layout. It will be argued that it is on a 'running-in/evaluation' trip!

Excursion set; any vacuum fitted engine(s) available. A Class 4F 0-6-0 or Horwich Mogul (2-6-0) would seem a good choice.

Plate 85 Freight trains are discussed in more detail later in the chapter but I have put this picture here to indicate the sort of thing which is so typical and which most modellers would not find beyond their resources. The picture was taken at Achnasheen on the Highland line to the Kyle and, although headed in BR days by a Stanier Class '5' 4-6-0, I guess that this train, in its time, has been hauled by anything from a 'Skye Bogie' to a BR Type '2' diesel. Nor do I suspect its nature changed very much either. This particular train is running under single line rules and the fireman can be seen leaning out with the tablet. The vehicles, some 17 in all, are a mixture of vans and open wagons with nothing really exotic at all. In earlier days it is likely that there would have been fewer vans in proportion. Note the cattle wagon immediately behind the tender, the old sleeping car in use as a dormitory carriage for staff and the usual bric-a-brac scattered about — all grist to the mill for the observant modeller (*Eric Treacy — courtesy P. B. Whitehouse*).

85

This may seem to be another somewhat tedious exercise; but it has two great virtues. Firstly it further emphasises, in the builder's mind, the 'mental' image of the type of railway which will emerge and secondly (probably more important) it serves to indicate quite clearly what sort of models should be tackled. This latter point can be critical on several grounds.

From the outset it can serve to indicate whether the building or acquisition programme is too ambitious in relation to cash and/or time scale envisaged. As a corollary, it can also point out where there may be purely modelling problems. These could vary from a lack of sufficient information about the prototype, via the realisation that there is a lack of suitable component parts for scratch-building, to sheer panic at the modelling difficulties involved! In the case of the modeller working from a 'ready-to-run' or 'kit' basis, it could reveal gaps in the offering from the trade or the total non-existence of an acceptable alternative. Whatever effect it may have, however, it will point out any difficulties and, even in the extreme case of forcing a few really major changes in overall plan and philosophy, it should save a lot of wasted time and expenditure in building or acquiring irrelevant models.

The same line of reasoning can and should be applied to freight patterns and traffic but I will not repeat the full detailed process of analysis. Rather, I will try to outline some of the basic principles behind freight service planning. Firstly, it is as well to remember that unless the modeller proposes to recreate a full main-line scene, there will be few, if any, really exotic specialised vehicles. Even on the main line they were quite rare. Thus, steer clear of train loads of specialised hopper wagons, plate and tube wagons, strings of bogie bolsters, high capacity brick wagons and many other types favoured by the ready-to-run and kit manufactures. What will be needed, assuming a typical steam-age scene characteristic of the 1900–60s period, are lots of open mineral wagons (mostly coal, of course), an almost equal number of assorted open merchandise wagons from one to five plank and a few covered vans. It is seldom realised how recently it is that vans rather than open wagons came to be widely used for merchandise. The 'sheeted-down' open wagon was far more common in pre-BR days.

On a typical secondary line, vacuum fitted freight stock would be quite rarely seen until quite late in the 'loose-coupled freight' era and would mostly be confined to 'perishable' cargoes (eg, fish, meat etc). In fact, almost as likely to appear as fitted freight vehicles would be items of non-passenger coaching stock attached, frequently, to stopping passenger trains. It often surprises me how rarely one sees milk vans, carriage trucks, horseboxes and the like on model railways — yet they were often more commonly seen around than fitted freight wagons. Incidentally, to avoid confusion, I use the phrase 'non-passenger coaching stock' to refer to any vehicle which was capable of operating attached to a passenger train. These types often appeared in the 'passenger coach' stock lists and very frequently carried passenger type numbers and liveries, or painting styles derived therefrom. The essence was that the automatic brake was continuous on the train — a rather minority occurrence on a pure freight train until well into BR days.

Additional to the above considerations should be an adequate supply of goods brake vans — at least one per train envisaged plus a few 'spares'. It was, of course, common for an in-coming freight to depart with the same brake van so there were never (proportionally) as many goods brakes dotted about doing nothing as normal freight wagons. However, this does raise the question of freight stock quantity overall.

It is hard to realise today, with block trains, intensive working, full train-load consignments etc, just how many freight vehicles in the old days were not actually moving at all. Local merchants would frequently use coal wagons, vans etc as 'free mobile warehouses' until such time as the railways insisted on having them back and, as a rough rule of thumb, for every vehicle in a train there would be at least one or more similar types standing idle. This had incredible ramifications in terms of siding provision and the modeller should try and provide as much siding space as his site will allow — and not mind if they get filled with vehicles! This of course, does allow the modeller to 'over-build' on the freight side, if he so wishes.

Nothing I have said should be taken to mean that unusual or more specialised vehicles *never* ventured onto secondary lines. The odd gunpowder van (for a quarry) or cattle wagons (on market day) would be the sort of thing which would often be seen.

More than the normal provisioning of 'non-coal' mineral or ballast wagons would be required if quarry traffic was featured. 'Loco' as opposed to 'domestic' coal wagons would obviously appear at motive power depots, as would ash-wagons. A steel works would merit plate, tube, bogie bolster and coil wagons; while other industries would require their own specialised vehicles. The essential thing here, as everywhere else, is to keep it relevant. Thus, in my own scheme, I shall include limestone wagons (for the quarries) cattle wagons and timber carrying vehicles to try to establish the local 'economic geography' of the model.

Chapter 7

Train formations and marshalling

Train marshalling seems to be an area where many modellers become confused. While they may well be able to work out how many and what sort of locomotives, carriages and wagons are needed to reproduce the bulk of the envisaged activity, there does not always seem to be the same degree of appreciation of the way in which trains were actually assembled. I am talking mainly of course, of the steam locomotive, vacuum braked age; but it did not change too much until fairly modern times.

If we are to consider the 1900–70 period as being likely to embrace the majority of potential historical railway models then the modeller should be aware of a few basic principles governing the way his trains should appear. There were, of course, rule books to follow on the real railway — and a copy of a relevant rule book can be a most useful document for the historical modeller — but a few overall generalisations can be identified. The first is that there is no better teacher than a historic photograph. I am constantly astonished how much can be gleaned by careful analysis of even a few pictures in terms of train make-up, types of vehicle, order of marshalling and so forth. From these it is possible to make 'intelligent guesses', if nothing better, when we assemble our model formations.

Turning first to passenger trains, the only vital factor is that there must be at least one handbraked vehicle for the guard to ride in. Every coach in the train itself is, of course, automatically braked throughout from the locomotive but the guard must have access to a place to ride and an emergency handbrake. There would also be luggage and parcels accommodation, in addition to that provided in the passenger carrying areas, and this was almost universally combined with the guard's and brake accommodation in a brake vehicle. This could vary from a 'full' brake (with no passenger seats) to a vehicle almost wholly composed of passenger carrying areas with but a minimum space for guard/brake/luggage. Whether or not vehicles had side corridors, lavatories or other exotica, was subsidiary.

Any train of more than two or three coaches would usually have two handbrake fitted vehicles and it was preferred to have these as end vehicles, brake ends outwards. However there were so many exceptions that 'inside-out' brakes and non-handbraked vehicles behind the brake van were common. Ideally, on the LMS at all events, no more than eight axles (ie, two bogie coaches) should have been marshalled to the rear of the brake vehicle — but there were often exceptions. In modelling terms this means that one brake will do for any train up to 5 vehicles provided it is placed somewhere in the middle. (NB modern BR loco-hauled Inter-City trains often have but one brake and they don't seem to mind whether it is front, back, or centre!)

Thus, the simplest train will consist of a prime mover with one carriage (I exclude single unit railcars), provided the latter has space for the guard etc. It is, therefore, perfectly legal to operate a locomotive and full brake and call it a 'parcels train'! Generally, however, more than one carriage was involved and more than one class of passenger accommodation. In this case, a useful rule of thumb is to keep first and third in proportions between 1:3 and 1:5. Excursions may be more dominantly third class (occasionally exclusively so), as were workmen's trains. Business expresses would often have proportionally more first class than, say, a cross-country local; but a Saturday only

Plates 86 to 89 *Express Trains* Express passenger trains were not always nice tidy rakes of carriages sharing a uniform profile — in fact, they were usually anything but — so I have selected a few examples covering a wide time-span to try to give a few more ideas to those who are trying to add more interest to their models.

The first picture shows a conventional pre-group Midland express — only six coaches be it noted! The engine is a Class '3' 4–4–0 and, in passing, some readers might like to note the further differences between this example (No 709) and the two later examples of the class analysed in detail in Plates 61 and 62. The train consists of clerestory corridors but they are a mixture of two or three types. The formation is quite typical. A brake composite leads (possibly a through carriage) followed by a five-coach section with brake at each end and a pair of massive dining cars in the middle. The types appear to be, from the front, brake third, third diner, first diner, third, brake composite. This sort of formation and length of train characterised the Midland main line almost to the outbreak of the Second World War. Change the engine to a Compound or '5XP' and the carriages to LMS standard types and you would have updated the concept by 20 years.

The second picture, taken at Chester c 1948, shows a Chester to Birkenhead train in early BR days. Several points can be made. Firstly, it is headed by a Stanier 2–6–0 No 42961, a type not often modelled and not often seen at the front of a train with express headlamps. Secondly the first three carriages are ex-GWR Siphon, ex-LNWR 50 ft or 52 ft 6 in corridor third and a Stanier composite. The rest of the train cannot be seen but there would have to be a brake somewhere. In modelling terms, it is workings like this which provide much more scope for copying than the glamorous named trains.

The Midland's small expresses are, of course, admirably suited to modellers but it is much more difficult when one comes to systems like the LNWR, GWR or East Coast route where longer trains were seen. Plate 88, taken at Euxton Junction c 1937–8 makes this point. 'Royal Scot' No 6136 *The Border Regiment* is pulling 11 bogies plus two milk tanks and a four-wheel van, the latter at the very rear. Few modellers could manage this, but look at the carriage types. Behind the milk tanks is an ex-LNWR full brake. The next six are LMS standards, but represent four distinct design types, and the last five consist of another full brake, three LMS corridors and, I suspect, a horse box. There are no dining cars and I would not be surprised if the train actually consists of two separate portions, joined together further north. Whatever the explanation, the main point of this picture is to show how much variety one can incorporate even as late as the 1930s and I feel quite certain there were many trains of five to seven vehicles or so, equally assorted, running under express headlamps on most British routes.

Finally, in this group of pictures, Plate 89 is a real oddity. Taken at Derby c 1949, it shows LMS design 2–6–2T No 41247 carrying express headlamps and pulling a train consisting, seemingly, of an ex-LNWR/WCJS six-wheel van plus a set of Stanier pattern non-corridors. It seems to demonstrate that there truly was a prototype for everything in steam days! (*D. Jenkinson collection, Eric Treacy — courtesy P.B. Whitehouse*).

86

89

Plates 90 to 97 *Local Passenger Trains* The very lifeblood of railway passenger operating was represented by the local, or stopping passenger train. In the last analysis, all that was literally needed was somewhere for the guard, somewhere for the passengers to travel and the correct locomotive headlamp code — one lamp below the chimney. The modelling possibilities are endless and in this group of pictures I have sorted out a few views which I would hope might spur the modeller's imagination. They are not all LMS, much less Settle and Carlisle.

The first view shows an impressive cross-country Midland train on the Leicester-Birmingham service near Wigston. Note that it is only one coach shorter than the MR express at Plate 86. The engine is a Kirtley 2–4–0 No 25 and the first three coaches are square-panelled clerestories, the second and third having lavatories. There follows one of the fairly rare MR elliptical roof non-corridors and a six-wheel clerestory van — a nice train for the modeller.

The next pair of pictures represent local passenger trains on the Settle and Carlisle but I have chosen to illustrate not the through service but that well-remembered train which diverted at Garsdale and went down the Hawes branch. Nicknamed 'Boniface', though no-one seems to know quite why, it was something of an institution in its day. The most common formation was of three coaches, two brake thirds plus composite, but the style of carriage varied. In the picture headed by Class '2' 4–4–0 No 459 (Plate 91) it has a Stanier brake third plus two slightly earlier LMS standards of the 1930–31 period; while in the picture showing Class '3' 2–6–2T No 183 (Plate 92) it consists wholly of ex-LNWR stock to a uniform profile. The pictures were taken c 1946 at Horton-in-Ribblesdale and Bell Busk respectively.

The 'three coach local' was, possibly, the most characteristic of all and most railways used them. The next picture (Plate 93) gives an ex-LNER example on the Grantham to Nottingham service in 1949. The engine is a former GER 4–6–0, rebuilt by Gresley (Class B12) and the train consists of an ex-GNR lavatory composite brake and a Gresley LNER articulated pair, (lavatory composite plus non-lavatory brake third, as far as can be seen). Finally, in the 'three coach' category, in Plate 94 a mid-1950s local is seen leaving Leeds City behind Class '4' 2–6–4T No 42412. The service is not identified but the train consists of ex-LYR brake third, ex-LMS standard composite and ex-LNWR third or brake third. The last carriage is not clear and it is just possible there was a fourth vehicle. If so and judging by the ecumenical nature of the first three carriages, it would be no great surprise if it turned out to be a Midland third brake!

92

93

94

It is not possible to get below one carriage but it is surprising how late into the BR period the one coach train survived. Frequently, but not always, it was motor-fitted, thus allowing the driver to control the train from the brake van of the coach in push-pull mode. A modern version of this concept was the pairing of the post-war Ivatt Class '2' 2–6–2T with a Stanier pattern trailer, exemplified in Plate 95 by No 41217 at Coniston in the 1950s. Dedicated modellers will have fun with all the additional plumbing on the front of the engine!

The alternative was a simple one-carriage locomotive-hauled operation in conventional mode and an interesting example is shown in Plate 96. The view was taken at Burnmouth (ex-North British Railway) in the early 1950s and shows the Eyemouth branch train in charge of Class 'J39' 0–6–0 No 64843. The carriage is a late LNER standard brake composite and the train is almost running in 'mixed train' mode, having two fitted vans behind the carriage.

Finally, and giving the lie to the earlier observation that one would not normally run big express power on three corridors, Plate 97 might bring consolation to the frustrated. It shows 'Royal Scot' No 46167 *The Hertfordshire Regiment* waiting in the northbound bay at Hellifield in the early 1960s with the mid-day local for Carlisle. The train consisted of three Stanier corridors, two brake seconds plus composite and during its final locomotive hauled life, prior to the introduction of DMUs in the late 1960s, could go up the 'Long Drag' behind anything that was to hand. I have personally seen it behind Class '5' 4–6–0s, 'Royal Scots', both types of BR standard 4–6–2s and even a Class '47' BR diesel-electric. (*NRM collection (3); Eric Treacy — courtesy P.B. Whitehouse (4); BR LMR*).

95

96

97

'extra' would have more third class. Where possible, the first class areas were marshalled fairly close together either somewhere in the centre of the train or exclusively at one end. A favourite LMS practice (since copied widely by BR, especially with the HSTs) was to put the first class at the 'London' end and separate this area from the third class by the catering facilities. (Nowadays, of course, one reads 'second' for 'third' class). If a train consisted of two or more sections, eg the LMS 'Royal Scot' then this sequence would be repeated viz:

first class
dining car(s) } for Edinburgh
third class
first class
dining car(s) } for Glasgow
third class

— each with its own brake vehicles.

A through carriage or carriages (usually comprising both classes and guard/brake accommodation) would be marshalled 'outboard', either front or rear, depending on the nature of the service; while any additional vehicles (to cope with extra traffic at peak periods) could go either 'outboard' or be inserted in the appropriate part of the train. Given a knowledge of these basic concepts, the modeller is probably best advised to work it out for himself, remembering that in essence, the purpose of assembling a set of carriages is to provide the right sort of facilities for the service in question — and there is plenty of scope for variety both in vehicle type (first, third, brake, composite, bogie, six-wheel etc) and vehicle period (pre-group, big four or BR).

To the main train there might be added parcels vans, milk vans, horseboxes, Post Office vehicles and the like. All that mattered was that the vehicles were compatible (in running terms) and that they reflected, as accurately as possible, the traffic requirement. There were even special rules relating to the odd occasions when non-automatically braked vehicles might (just) be permitted on passenger trains.

98

99

Plates 98 and 99 *Parcels Trains* From the modelling point of view, parcels trains are almost as good as freight trains — moreover, being essentially composed of covered vehicles, the question of loading and unloading does not confuse the issue. All that matters is that the vehicles should be 'passenger rated' — see text — and should include at least one vehicle with guard and brake accommodation. Two splendid examples are given here and I am certain that they represent the same train on different occasions. They were both taken at Holbeck (low level) on the Midland line to Bradford from Leeds in the early 1950s and show broadly similar formation. Essentially, the trains consist of full brakes (at least one), milk tanks and four-wheeled vans. Note also that they run under their own headcodes — see Appendix III — and were frequently put in charge of passenger engines rather than freight types. The locomotives are Class '2' 4–4–0 No 40362 and Compound Class '4' 4–4–0 No 41107 respectively.

Modellers should bear in mind that the railways possessed a very large number of vehicles in this category and that for a layout to be convincing it should incorporate a fair representation of these very characteristic types (*Eric Treacy — courtesy P.B. Whitehouse*).

Plate 100 This picture shows a somewhat specialised form of working which also ran under 'parcels' headcode. It is in fact that fast vanishing phenomenon — or has it gone already? — the milk train. This one has Settle and Carlisle connections because it is seen passing the one-time rail connected milk depot at Appleby, from whence it undoubtedly obtained the bulk, if not all of its load. On this occasion a freight engine is in charge (Class '8F' No 48283). Note the full brake in the mid part of the train for the guard (*H.L. Overend — courtesy NRM*).

On the freight side, all that was necessary was a prime mover and a goods brake to accompany the cargo carrying vehicles. The goods brake was always the last vehicle but the question of automatic braking of all vehicles from the engine rarely arose until more recent years. The engine could brake itself; and the guard applied the handbrake in the guard's van to control the train. The cargo vehicles themselves had handbrakes. These were used mostly as parking brakes in sidings (after shunting); but at the top of the steeper gradients, out on the line, hand-brakes were also applied (on all or some of the vehicles) to add additional stopping power to that of the engine and guard's van.

As automatic brakes were fitted to goods vehicles, a few additional rules began to apply — and these do affect model train marshalling. On the main line, express freight trains with a proportion of vehicles fitted with automatic brakes would have all such vehicles immediately behind the locomotive, their brakes connected to the locomotive and applied by the driver. This was known as the 'fitted head' of the train and, even if it only consisted of a few vehicles, could considerably enhance the brake power available to the driver and allow the train to

be run at an enhanced speed. A fully fitted freight (a very rare creature indeed until after the Second World War) could be operated at even higher speed so the railways tended to concentrate their meagre supply of fitted vehicles into fully or partially fitted trains to speed up the traffic flows — and not surprisingly, fitted vehicles tended to be confined to high value types of traffic (or perishables) where transit speed mattered.

However, the 'pick-up freight' — the train

Plates 101 to 106 *Freight Trains* During the bulk of the steam era, the freight train generated more revenue for the railways than passenger workings — and there are many experts who consider that it is impossible for any railway to operate profitably or properly unless it hauls freight in greater value than passenger traffic (BR please note!). The consequence of this is that unless the modeller is reproducing one of the *specialised* passenger lines, freight traffic must play a prominent part. Moreover, there is more sheer operating potential in freight working as far as modelling is concerned. The essential ingredient is the local freight, as discussed in the main text, but once the main line services are considered, then again we are in the area of categorisation. The accompanying pictures attempt to cover some of these categories.

The first type illustrated is the so-called 'through freight' which was by far the most common main line goods train of the steam period. In LMS days, it covered virtually anything which ran more than 15 miles without stopping and could include almost any type of vehicle or cargo. The first example shows the classic form — LMS Class '4F' No 4190 leaving Rise Hill tunnel on the Settle-Carlisle c 1946. the train seems to be a mixture of orthodox wagons and vans, many of the former being sheeted down. If there are any fitted vans, they will be part of the first group of four but, if so, the train should be running under express freight headlamps — see Appendix III — unless, of course, the vacuum brake is not in use.

The second example (Plate 102) shows a somewhat similar train at Wavertree c 1937, headed, somewhat unusually, by a 'Prince of Wales' type ex-LNWR 4–6–0 No 25804 and there are certainly no fitted vehicles at the front of this one. The 'Prince of Wales' Class was, of course, very numerous on the ex-LNWR lines and quite an effective mixed traffic engine before the Class '5' came along in quantity; but in freight terms it would, possibly, be more likely to be seen on fitted or parcels traffic. Even so, however, it gives more scope to the modeller.

The last example selected with the 'one over one' headlamp code looks for all the world like a mineral train (see Appendix III), being composed entirely of open mineral wagons (Plate 103). Presumably it was travelling more than 15 miles without scheduled stops and at slightly higher speed — very many 'solid coal' trains ran on both the LMS and BR with through freight classification. The train is waiting in the up loop at Blea Moor and may have taken water as well. No doubt an express, or some such, was due and one of the most characteristic forms of railway operating is represented here, known as putting freight 'inside' to wait for faster traffic to overtake. The date is c 1946 and the engine No 8177, a Stanier Class '8F' 2–8–0.

The next category upwards in long distance goods traffic was the express freight which could carry fitted vehicles at its head. It would generally be travelling further and also a little faster but was frequently indistinguishable visibly from the more numerous through freights. Plates 104 and 105 clearly show this, both from the Settle and Carlisle. The earlier example in Plate 104 shows Class '3F' 0–6–0 No 3287 on a mixed assortment of vans and wagons and it is possible that the first few vehicles are fitted. If so, it might have been running as a so-called 'Maltese' freight because of the Maltese cross symbol used in the working timetable to distinguish them from other express freights — see Appendix III. The date is c 1938, but it could have been almost any time from the 1920s to the mid-1960s, so little did matters change.

This fact is well exemplified by Plate 105 showing an ex-WD 2–8–0 No 90335, topping Ais Gill summit with a southbound express freight, well into BR days. If there is a fitted 'head' at all it consists of the solitary cattle wagon!

The undoubted aristocrat of steam age freight in Britain was the fully fitted train and the LNER even built a class of engines, the 'V2' 2–6–2s, to handle this traffic and named the class after the crack goods service from Kings Cross to the north — 'Green Arrow'. The LMS did not quite go to this extent but fitted freights were often given passenger engines, even after the Class '5' 4–6–0 was available in quantity. Such a situation is shown at Plate 106 with Compound 4–4–0 No 1069 appearing to have no trouble at all with a southbound fitted as it approaches Ais Gill summit in the summer of 1939. Note the fact that, alone of the trains illustrated in this section, there are no open wagons.

Fully fitted trains did not necessarily have every single vehicle vacuum braked and readers should study Appendix III to appreciate the more subtle points of these, and other, freight trains (*NRM collection — 5; Eric Treacy — courtesy P. B. Whitehouse*).

103

104

which merely collected or delivered wagons from intermediate stations to take them to or from marshalling yards, was often operated by a locomotive not even equipped with automatic vacuum brake. In this case, the fitted vehicles were treated like any others and often added to the train at random. Loaded cattle wagons were marshalled next to the engine (to avoid over much injury to the livestock in the see-saw motion of a freight train) and gunpowder and petroleum wagons tended to go to the rear (but never immediately next to the guard!) for obvious reasons.

At the main marshalling yard(s), the various pick-up freights from outlying areas were sorted by destination but with the fitted vehicles forming one group at the front and the non-fitted stock coming behind in the outgoing express and through freight trains made up in the yards. Additionally, when fitted or partially fitted freights became more common and train speeds increased, the railways then considered axleboxes more carefully. In steam days, there were two sorts of freight axlebox, those lubricated with grease (almost solid when cool) and those lubricated by oil. Grease (or 'fat') boxes were the older standard and relied on the friction of the axle end rotating within the axlebox to warm-up and melt the semi-solid grease and thus lubricate the bearings. Oil boxes were much better in that the lubricant was always liquid, provided better lubrication and the wagons could be run at higher speeds. This difference did not matter too much when all freights were slow speed and non-fitted, but, as automatic brakes came into use on even a few vehicles, thus permitting higher speeds, the grease box vehicles could run too hot if speeds got too high.

In consequence, the railways began to exclude grease box vehicles from their higher speed freights and, as a rough rule of thumb, it would not normally be prototypical to operate, on a model, a main line freight with a fitted head *and* grease box non-fitted wagons to the rear ... although I have no doubt that it *did* happen! I will not go into the additional ramifications caused by 'through pipe' vehicles save to say that these, while having a vacuum pipe fitted from one end to the other, were without their own automatic brakes. They did allow the continuous vacuum to be maintained between automatically braked vehicles (on either side) and could go in the middle of a fitted head, sometimes even on passenger trains, subject to strict rules. It is quite useful to know this since many cattle wagons were equipped with a through pipe (but not vacuum braked) to enable them to go behind the locomotive without destroying the fitted head, thus permitting livestock traffic to participate in the faster transit times afforded by the presence of fully fitted stock. Sometimes, through pipe vehicles are referred to as 'partially fitted'.

It is for the modeller to try to assess the likely characteristics of his freight trains and marshall them accordingly. In general, main line trains will have their vehicles assembled by destination, as will inward bound local freights. The precise order of marshalling for each destination will depend on the siding layout to be shunted. The principle was to minimise shunting moves and could involve some vehicles being at the rear, others at the front, bearing in mind the over-riding rules regarding brakes etc. Outward bound local and pick-up freights, save for single cargo consignments (eg, cattle specials, coal trains etc,) would present a somewhat random mix — it being left to the principal marshalling yards to get matters sorted out more rationally. The daily pick-up would do the least amount of shunting possible to attach/detach vehicles if for no other reason than that constantly reversing the locomotive was quite tiring work for the driver, not to mention the extra operation of the points either by the signalman or, if hand operated, the lineside shunter himself, or even the guard or fireman.

In a definitive historical model there is considerable scope for operational subtlety combined with authentic movements and marshalling. The subject as a whole well repays study (through photographs etc) and nicely sets the scene for the next chapter.

Chapter 8

Model railway operation

'Carriage Trucks and Horseboxes are kept at all the principal stations on the line; but to prevent the possibility of disappointment it is recommended that one day's notice be given at the stations when they are required'.

Midland Railway Public Timetable, 1903

The only trouble with a statement like the above is that it does not define 'principal station'! However, it is one of many such official exhortations (to railway staff and public alike) which should, ultimately, be reflected in the appearance of our model layouts in terms of vehicles provided and the operation thereof. Yet, considering that most modellers go to considerable pains to make their creations move under their own power, it is a constant source of surprise to me how little attention they pay to the operational fidelity of their systems. For every layout which is operated as though railwaymen were in charge, there must be half a dozen or more on which movement is random, unreliable and illogical.

As far as I am concerned, the operation of a model railway can only be seen as that which adds authentic train movement to an already, hopefully convincing, static scene. I have explained earlier that realism will always be somewhat limited because certain parts of the scene must always remain static; but realistic train movement is possible. This almost inevitably necessitates operating to timetable or sequence rather than simply letting a train charge round the system time after time. The latter can be appealing, as I have already hinted, but it is not really operation in the sense of inceasing the credibility of a historical scene; so I do not propose to mention it again.

'Real' operating involves a fundamental understanding of the ways of the railway. For those of us who are old enough to recall the pre-modern image period, we have our own memories and experiences to help; but I must own that for many younger enthusiasts (probably most of those born after nationalisation) who have a genuine wish to re-create a former period of railway history, it is difficult to know what to do or where to start. An old copy of the General Appendix to the working timetables of the company modelled is a very useful start and gives a welter of valuable detail; but these books are not as easily come by as was once the case. Normal libraries are unlikely to have them and many modellers will have to rely on other sources for most of their knowledge. It is principally to these people that my comments in this section are addressed and I hope that those readers who can recall former days will forgive me for stating what might, to them, seem obvious. Perhaps a slight digression will help to demonstrate my reasoning.

A few years ago I was at a model railway exhibition whereat a young man (mid-teenage I guess) was operating a rather nice little branch line, stocked mainly with proprietary items lettered 'LMS'. There was a goodly scatter of private owner wagons and appropriate stock, the young man had set his scene extremely well and was shunting the goods yard quite nicely. He eventually despatched a freight train but forgot, as I at first supposed, to attach the brake van. I said 'You have forgotten the brake van.' He replied, quite innocently, 'What is a brake van?.' When I took a further look I realised that there was no brake van on the layout and when I continued the discussion it transpired that the only real-life freight trains the young

109

Plates 107 to 109 These three pictures could well have been included elsewhere in the book — they would serve to illustrate many of the points I have been emphasising — but they seemed to me to fit here since they seem to encapsulate the whole business of the 'total railway' and its operation. They have been deliberately chosen from but one part of the country, in this case, the former Highland Railway, in order to show just how much variation one could observe even within one quite modest system.

The first view shows a typical(!) local train in the days just after the grouping. The formation and origin of the coaches simply defy all logical analysis but no doubt there was some good reason why this magnificent array of semi-museum pieces and modern vehicles was setting off for Inverness behind No 14691 *Brodie Castle*. In an earlier chapter I mentioned the word 'atmosphere' and this picture serves to remind me that our modelling efforts are at their best if we can create scenes which are as evocative as this one — and operation of models is just as much about creating atmosphere as anything else.

In marked contrast to the first scene is the charming view, in Plate 108, of a diminutive 4–4–0T No 15014 a few years later at Strathpeffer Spa. This is a real mixed train with both passenger and goods brake accommodation and yet, I venture to suggest, if something like this were to appear on a model layout purporting to represent the LMS, many people would greet it with disbelief; as indeed they might the last of this group (Plate 109), were it not more recent in history. This one shows the train which served the Dornoch branch in the early 1950s — an elderly 0–4–4T plus one modern corridor composite brake and odd vans as required. Sadly, such trains are no longer to be seen in this country but this picture serves to remind us that they lasted much longer than might be supposed and could well be operated on a model layout representing quite recent practice (*Gavin Wilson collection — all*).

man had seen were the modern BR versions, fully braked and without a brake van! I hope I managed to explain how and why these things were different in LMS days and, should he read this book, I hope he is pleased that he has provided the inspiration for the next few pages.

The time factor

I think it is necessary to develop a realistic conception of the meaning of speed in railway terms. In the modern 125 mph HST days, with even many of the freight trains racing along at what seem to me to be obscene 70–80 mph speeds, it is difficult to realise how slowly, relatively speaking, things actually moved in the steam age. I know that *Mallard* reached 126 mph (once and very briefly), but the railway as a whole, at that time, was a 60–70 mph sort of affair even for the best trains; while normal freight trains (with a very few highly favoured exceptions) were doing very well indeed if they managed to cover 20 or 30 miles in one hour. Local passenger trains occasionally reached the heights of 60 mph (given enough distance between stations) but the pick-up freights were doing well if they ambled along between stops at 15–25 mph. There would even be time for the fireman, if he was so minded, to stop and pick dandelions for his rabbits off a lineside cutting before the signalman at the next block post began to show undue concern about the whereabouts of the train!

That this is true was borne home to me forcefully in mid-1983 when I was involved with helping to operate Stanier 4–6–2 *No 46229, Duchess of Hamilton* from Carlisle back to York. An immense load, by steam standards, of some 570 tons had been hung on the back of our locomotice and the engine was making a magnificent attack on the 1 in 100 uphill Appleby to Ais Gill section at 48–50 mph. All that one customer could say was that it 'seemed a bit slow'! The fact that the engine was delivering almost 3,000 hp at the cylinders and performing better than any single unit BR diesel could possibly have done (save, perhaps for a 'Deltic' in good order) was completely overlooked. This chap was obviously brainwashed with 4,500 hp of HST power cars on some 250 tons of lightweight Mk III stock on the dead level sections of the East Coast main line!

Thus, the first thing to do, in terms of historically authentic operating, is to 'slow everything down'. This can be even slower than one might suppose — and the very few layouts which operate at what I might call scale speed are often criticised for being *too* slow. However, consider for a moment a few facts. At 60 mph, a real train covers 88 ft per second. In 4 mm scale terms this is just under 14 in per second (7 mm equivalent, $24\frac{1}{2}$ in per second). At 90 mph (an almost unattainable speed most of the time in steam days), the figures are 21 in per second and 37 in per second respectively. Alternatively, a characteristic freight train at 30 mph would cover only 7 in per second in 4 mm scale and about 12 ins, in Gauge 'O'. Next time you operate your layout, try to run the trains at these sort of speeds and I wager that most of you will be surprised to see what real scale speed is all about.

As for shunting, anything much above a brisk walking speed (say 5 mph) would be very quick most of the time. This is no more than $1\frac{1}{2}$ in per second in 4 mm scale, $2\frac{1}{2}$ in per second, in 7 mm; from which it should follow that *good slow running* is a prerequisite of authentic model operation. Moreover, it should take just as long to marshal the trains in miniature as it does in reality — and this brings me to the subject of so-called 'scale time'.

It is often assumed that because we can reduce the physical dimensions of our models, related to reality, we can also reduce the time taken to carry out operations. This is philosophically nonsensical. If it is necessary for a real locomotive to take say, four seconds to travel its own length, then it must also take the same time to perform the same operation in miniature — unless we want our models to twitch around like frightened rabbits! I would go so far as to state, as a totally unassailable precept, that it is impossible to scale the time factor. In consequence, if you have worked out a 24 hour timetable for your railway along the lines I have suggested then it will take precisely 24 hours to run it, if everything is to be carried out properly!

This, of course, is unacceptable to most modellers who, maybe, have only two or three hours available at any one time. Moreover, on a real railway, much time is occupied between trains when nothing physically moves at all for many hours at a time. Office work is done, vehicles are loaded/unloaded and so on, but the trains do not move at all. For the onlooker of the miniature system, this is a crashingly boring situation — two real hours of no activity at the miniature equivalent of 2:30 pm! Speeding up the clock does not really solve the problem so I have evolved a modellers' compromise. On my models, I attempt to carry out all manoeuvres in 'real time' terms but I suppress, totally, the intervals between separate activities. Thus if, for example, the timetable shows no train action between 2:00 pm and 4:00 pm, then I go straight from 2:00 pm to 4:00 pm in the operational sequence and do not get too neurotic about the 'lost' two hours.

In practice I have discovered that if one allows one minute (real time) to represent five minutes (prototype time), then one can actually perform the specific manoeuvres at realistic visual speeds and absorb all the prototypical 'dead' time in the process. Thus, my operational schedule starts, notionally, at about 4:30 am with the arrival of the overnight sleeping cars (see timetable, page 97) and concludes, just after midnight, with the departure of the same carriages — a 'prototype' time of about 20 hours. I find that this can be performed in just under four hours at scale speeds, provided that each scheduled activity follows immediately after the previous one.

This is not, perhaps, an ideal solution but it works and I know of no other alternative which, on the one hand, enables a complete sequence to be operated in a reasonable 'real time' envelope and on the other, permits the physical movements to take place at a realistic pace from the onlooker's viewpoint.

If the logic of the previous paragraphs is acceptable to the reader, then the next stage is to analyse the nature of the train operations themselves and I will tackle these in four areas namely, passenger, freight, locomotive and signalling. At all times I shall be taking as my model a typical steam age scene, which remained, in essence, very stable in its general principles from the turn of the century to the mid-1960s — and there is still quite a lot of similar activity on the BR lines of the 1980s.

Passenger train operations

I make no secret of the fact that the subject of passenger trains and their operation is my own particular favoured area. This is partly because, in many ways, it is a neglected part of the model scene but also because I find it fascinating in its own right. Most modellers seem to accept, almost instinctively, that freight traffic demands attention, but tend not to take the same view with passenger services. All that ever seems to happen is that a train arrives, the engine runs round and then departs again — no problem. The reality is a little different. Firstly, all passenger stock is continuously braked and therefore, when shunting coaches, the train brake pipe has to be made and proved (ie tested for completion and efficiency). This involves checking the vacuum pipe connections between all the separate carriages and ensuring that the last one (at the rear of the

Plate 110 At the time this picture was taken, it was difficult to model authentic passenger trains unless one was prepared to make the carriages oneself. This was my own first effort at 'Boniface' (Plates 91 and 92) as I felt it might have looked in the mid-1930s. I cannot be *sure* that it utilised Midland clerestories (or, for that matter, that it did not) but I chose to build a reasonable Midland set. Only a few months later there were kits available! (*Roy Anderson*).

110

111

Plate 111 My 7 mm scale models have been built from the outset with the operating requirement of the layout in mind and this picture, taken when 'Kendal Mk I' was only some six months into construction, shows the bulk of my supposed through train from St Pancras. A view from the opposite end is given at Plate 47 and the formation, back from the engine is brake third, third, third open diner, first diner, composite and brake composite. Since the picture was taken I have decided to replace the composite with a brake first and regard the brake composite as a through coach from Bristol. It is not a very big express but is quite in line with Midland line practice — see, for example, Plates 71 and 86 (*Ron Prattley*).

train) is sealed into its housing. The same is true for the steam heat and/or Westinghouse brake pipes if fitted. On electrically lit stock it is also common for electrical plug/socket connections to be made between carriages to allow the guard to control all the train lighting from one point. Finally, all the screw couplings have to be tightened to bring the side buffers into firm contact.

With a corridor train made of vehicles with the old British Standard gangways (mostly confined to the LMS and GWR) it was also necessary to unfasten the retaining hooks (which restrained the collapsible part of the gangways by keeping them fully compressed to the carriage end) thus allowing the bellows section to be pulled outwards to meet the similar gangway on an adjacent vehicle. The two 'free' ends had to be clipped to each other to avoid accidents to passengers passing through. Endboards were then clipped to the extreme outer ends of the formation to seal them off.

Of course, with buckeye couplers and

Pullman-type gangways (LNER, SR and nowadays BR) the mere act of propelling two vehicles together will make the coupling and seal the gangway. But all the pipes etc, still need connections and if, for example, an LMS coach was gangwayed to an LNER coach then the former had to be fitted with gangway adapters (to allow clipping to the LNER gangway) and the LNER vehicle would have to have its buckeye coupler dropped out of the way (to expose a normal coupling hook) and its side buffers extended. In practice, a degree of loose coupling of coaches was often tolerated in the carriage sidings during the train make-up stage. But before an assembled set of vehicles was despatched to the station for traffic purposes, and certainly before loading any passengers, all the necessary connections had to be made and tested. Needless to say, all these processes had also to be undertaken when attaching or detaching vehicles to and from passenger rated trains. This would, therefore, also apply to mail and parcels trains and, likewise, to the fitted head of any freight train.

These operations took time to complete and the implications, for modellers, are that this time should be reproduced in some way. The sado-masochist might actually try to make models wherein all the pipework etc, is properly modelled and connected together! It can be done, especially in 7 mm scale, but for most normal mortals the best substitute is a rational pause between movements.

Thus, to take a simple run-round operation by way of example, the following sequence is correct:

a) The incoming train arrives and stops with a full automatic brake application. The coaches are now braked and even if the brake pipe is not broken, it cannot again move until a new vacuum is created.

b) Head/tail lamps are removed and if the engine can be run round without moving the train it can now be uncoupled, allowing due time to disconnect brake/heat pipes, unscrew the coupling (possibly easing back the locomotive to compress the buffers to assist this process). If the locomotive has to move the train before the run round pointwork is cleared, then time must be allowed to recreate the vacuum in the train pipe and release the brakes, which are applied again when the train is in the correct position.

c) The locomotive (now a light engine) moves up beyond the release crossover and waits until it receives a signal to set back. This also takes time (point changing, ground or shunting signals, locomotive reversing gear etc.)

d) The locomotive now sets back and starts the run round procedure but it may have to stop before it completes the manoeuvre if the pointwork at the rear of the train (soon to become the front) is under the control of a different signal box, ground frame or whatever.

e) The locomotive completes the run round and stops. Again time must be allowed to change the points and signals and reverse the locomotive (a screw reverse gear will take longer than a lever reverse).

f) The locomotive moves slowly onto the

Plate 112 One thing which modellers can do to enhance the operation of their layouts is to arrange the odd 'special' train, either passenger or freight. The fact that it runs every time the layout operates is largely irrelevant! The example here is a horsebox special from the GWR being worked up the Lickey incline by a Johnson MR 4–4–0 No 304. This could have been in connection with a race meeting or similar event and the train also carries a single passenger coach for the guard and some of the staff. The grooms rode in the horseboxes and on the Midland/LMS at least, were not classified as passengers! (*NRM collection*).

train and gently buffers-up. Remember that in reality, there may well be passengers in the train so 'softly-softly' is the watchword.

g) Brake/heat pipes etc. are re-connected, along with the couplings and a new vacuum created and proved. Head/tail lamps are re-positioned.

h) The train is now ready to depart on receipt of the appropriate signal.
This is quite a lot of activity for one of the simplest possible railway routines.

In modelling terms, the only way to reproduce this is with pauses — which is why the unknowing observer may well wonder what on earth is going on and accuse the layout operator of carrying out activities too slowly. There's not much one can do about this save grin and bear it, or try to explain the reasoning.

I will not waste space by analysing in similar detail all the other possible operations regarding passenger trains — I would hope that readers will be able to work it out for themselves. As part of Appendix III, I have given the basic definitions of passenger rated

trains in accordance with LMS practice in the 1930s, along with their locomotive head-lamp and signal bell codes. When to this are added all the specific regulations regarding passenger stock marshalling, the time-consuming nature of the operations is only too easy to appreciate. In fact, one wonders sometimes how they ever managed to cope at all. It is therefore worth noting that one of the reasons why the railways prefer to use fixed 'sets' of carriages is in order to reduce the time taken to make and break train formations — and this is as true today with air-braked BR Mk III stock as it was in former times. In fact, it is probably more true today than ever. Separate through-portions of trains are, nowadays, very rare and when did you last see modern BR operators add the odd extra carriage or two to cope with peak loading? They will tell you that it is not possible, especially with HST formations; but this is rubbish. It is still perfectly possible to 'strengthen' trains, even HSTs if necessary, and operate separate through carriages; but the economics are, apparently,

Plate 113 I could not resist including this picture since it seems to me the prototype version of the modeller's operational nightmare! It was taken at Agecroft in 1926 (ex-L&YR) and most tracks seem packed full of wagons and locomotives. It does, however, emphasise the point made elsewhere about the number of wagons to be seen standing around. Note the considerable variety of lettering styles in this early post-grouping view — a useful point for modellers of this period who wish to retain pre-group liveries (*Real Photographs*).

not acceptable in modern circumstances. In consequence the 'modern image' modeller does not have to worry quite as much as his historical counterpart.

Freight train operations

The next aspect to consider is freight train operation. I have already explained something of the ramifications in this area and, in modelling terms, the proper operation of freight traffic can be one of the most rewarding areas of the hobby. However, it must be done in a logical way.

As part of Appendix III I have given, as with passenger trains, a basic summary of the various categories of freight train recognised by the LMS, along with their headlamp and signalling bell codes; but for model purposes I think a more important aspect than merely having an encyclopaedic knowledge of the rule book, useful though this may be, is to ensure that the trains themselves relate properly to the geographical reality of the area modelled as explained in the previous chapter. Only when this is achieved does it make sense to look at the rules to discover what precise sort of train would be most appropriate to the traffic on offer.

Having resolved this matter, which will differ from system to system, we can then, and only then, decide how to actually operate the vehicles on the layout. In a nutshell, the word is 'purposefully'. At all times one must try to remember that we are striving for an illusion of reality. It might be fun to bang a few wagons into and out of sidings as often as possible in order to demonstrate the superb slow running capabilities of our favourite shunting locomotive — but the real railways do not do this. The object is to get the job done as quickly as possible in as few moves as possible.

The reason is not hard to seek because in reality the job is hard work. It involves constant reversal of the locomotive — a tiresome job in steam days especially if it was fitted with screw reverse gear necessitating many turns of the reversing wheel (or handle) from full forward to full backward gear. It involves much coupling and uncoupling of vehicles with that fearsome instrument, the shunter's pole. It can involve pinning down (or unpinning) handbrakes, or the making/breaking of vacuum pipe and/or screw coupling connections. It can involve much manipulation of hand operated point levers, or much to-ing and fro-ing in the

signal box if the points are connected to the lever frame. Thus, the least effort expended, the better it is for all concerned.

In practical terms this means working out, before any movement starts, the order in which the train should be marshalled to minimise shunting movements. As part of my job, I have actually sat in the brake van with a goods guard for ten or fifteen minutes or more in order to work out complex movements at the Railway Museum sidings before starting the shunt. It is time well spent and its miniature equivalent is perfectly possible.

At its simplest, if the train to be made up is assumed to be destined for a nearby marshalling yard where it will be sorted (possibly over a hump), along with many other similar trains, into express and through freights for various major destinations, the likelihood is that the vehicles will be marshalled as they come, save for ensuring that livestock/fitted vehicles are properly treated. Thus, apart from ensuring that there is a brake van at the rear, nothing much need be added. Such a train — variously referred to as a 'pick-up', 'local' or 'trip' working — was the very lifeblood of railway freight operation, the seed corn out of which the main line services grew. As it proceeded from station to staion it would gradually collect the outward bound traffic and by the time it reached destination could have assumed both massive and very random characteristics — or, on a quiet day, it could hardly seem worth the effort of running it at all.

The next complication is if the train is destined both to collect and deliver en route. Here it would be normal to separate vehicles for an intermediate location from those due to go the whole distance. Whether the intermediate traffic went front or rear would depend on the nature of the various sidings to be shunted on the way. Sometimes it may be sensible to place some vehicles at the front, others (for a different destination) at the rear. All depends on keeping the inevitable shunting movements to a minimum. This basic pattern of activity can be taken just as far as the modeller wishes. Our American friends are rather better at it than we are, if truth be told. At the very least, each wagon in a yard should be assigned a destination before the start of an operating session. This can be as simple as 'go' or 'stay' or as complex as giving a specific terminal point for every wagon and imposing restrictions as to total loads, type of train by which to be consigned, priority

114

115

116

Plates 114 and 115 These two pictures show unusual trains which would be well within the scope of many modelmakers and would not look out of place on quite a number of layout types. They would certainly add to the operational potential. The first example shows a breakdown train of the kind which many railways kept ready for action at larger depots. This one is the ex-L&YR train based at Newton Heath in 1931. It consists, essentially, of riding and tool vans, the crane itself and the crane 'runners' which went below the jib of the crane when in transit. It would be unlikely that many layouts would have an MPD big enough for a permanent breakdown train but if there was one available on the layout (say in the storage area), it would certainly add to the operational complications if whenever there was a derailment, the breakdown train had to be despatched to the scene before routine services could be resumed!

The second view shows an idea which I have never seen modelled but which would serve as a useful conversation piece if nothing else. It shows a former LYR 0–8–0 carrying stopping freight headlamps leaving Agecroft in 1930. The main payload is a brand new LMS 'Garratt'. Now most of us have at least one motor-less locomotive! (*G. Coltas, A. G. Ellis*).

Plate 116 This view of 'Garsdale Road' sums up in model form some of the operational points which can be tackled in model form. The main lines are clear but No 3893 is obviously pulling out onto the main, being beyond the turnout leading to the yard. The track gang are in a static situation, since trains are moving, so their immobility is acceptable, as is that of the locomotive driver with his elbow on the cabside. Finally, the loaded minerals in the lay-by suggest that something is about to happen on the up main line (*Brian Monaghan*).

handling characteristics and so on. The back issues of model magazines should prove a source of guidance here and I do believe this is one area where the individual modeller must decide for himself.

However, when it finally comes to moving the vehicles around the layout itself, the same principles hold as for shunting passenger trains. First of all keep it very slow — remember that in reality real men have to perform operations which can be highly dangerous if loose coupled wagons are allowed to career around at high speed all over the place, or if operation is careless. As a somewhat sombre aside, I was actually present when a shunter was killed in such an incident and since my job sometimes involves my presence during shunting operations with loose coupled vehicles, I have learned the value of attention to detail in these matters.

It does show when a layout is operated on these principles and I will conclude this section by recounting two anecdotes about my own modelling activities which I hope bear this out. The first goes back to 'Marthwaite' days in the mid 1960s. We used proper bell codes (see Appendix III) and a freight train was offered to Marthwaite from the storage area. The operator at the terminus acknowledged the bell code and then did nothing at all! Amongst the spectators were a couple of visitors, one of whom was

obviously baffled. He said, audibly, to his companion: 'Why haven't they brought that train in yet?'. His friend replied: 'You silly fool, it's supposed to have set off some five miles down the line. It takes time for it to get here and they are allowing "time on the block"'. We were delighted!

The second tale concerns 'Garsdale Road'. We were exhibiting at Leeds Corn Exchange and it was the custom of the railwaymen from Holbeck (the ex-LMS/Midland shed at Leeds for those who are unfamiliar with the area) to come along in their off duty periods. My layout was supposed to represent a bit of the line which these men operated regularly so we always tried to be on our toes. Now one of the sequences involved shunting the pick-up freight against the knowledge that there was a main line mineral train close on its heels. The object was to clear the main line without appearing to rush matters, before the minerals were offered, otherwise the latter may have to stop.

Plate 117 This was something of a posed picture, taken originally to show proper loads on wagons and the fact that vacuum fitted vans could quite reasonably be attached to passenger trains; but as a static view of 'Garsdale Road' it seems to suggest activity and movement, helped by the fact that No 65 has already passed the starter — in other words it is moving (*Roy Anderson*).

Plate 118 Ten years after this picture was taken, I cannot remember whether we ran this train as a parcels or 'fully fitted' but I think it was the former. Most vehicles were non-passenger coaching stock and we tried to simulate the 'fitted' nature of the service by running the train considerably faster than the rest of the freight service — and it seemed to come off. I say 'we' in reference to my long suffering friends who helped to operate this layout (*Brian Monaghan*).

On one occasion, the pick-up was not quite clear when the minerals were offered — a not unusual real-life situation. The mineral was started from the storage roads at very slow speed in the hope that it could manage to creep up to the 'home' signal but still give time for the pick-up to clear the main line. The reasoning was that, in reality, no main line freight driver of a heavy loose-coupled mineral train would actually stop his train if he could keep it moving forward, however slowly, after sighting an adverse 'distant' signal. Thus it was that the mineral train came creeping round the corner, inch by inch, while we got the pick-up out of the way. We were so absorbed in getting it right that we did not notice that a couple of our Holbeck friends had arrived (a driver and his fireman) until suddenly, the driver called out, having seen the main line train — 'Sithee, he's a cautious bugger isn't he? But its better than having to stop with all that load'. If you can persuade *real* railwaymen to suspend belief that they are looking at a model, then you are well on the way!

Locomotive operations

It is not by coincidence that I have relegated locomotive operations to third place after dealing with passenger and freight matters. The job of the railway is to move traffic and only when traffic needs are known can we look at both the locomotive requirement and how to deal with it.

The type of locomotive(s) we select should, where possible, be appropriate to the job required. One need not be too specific here as there is ample scope for the modeller to indulge his personal preferences. In general I would recommend that the selection of motive power should lean towards that which typifies rather than to the more exotic, albeit theoretically feasible, types, especially if historical veracity is to be enhanced. However, the most unlikely engines have appeared on quite improbable trains in their time so one need not be too dogmatic.

It is much more important to ensure that the locomotive provisioning and the servicing facilities associated with it, are appropriate. We all like engine sheds (or motive power depots (MPD) to use the LMS term) and most modellers, self included, do their level best to justify such a feature. However we should really ask ourselves; 'Does this sort of place really need a full-blown locomotive depot or would a turntable and water column suffice?'. My initial plans for Kendal (see Fig 18) envisaged a pretty impressive MPD and it was only when I fully analysed

the traffic pattern and stock requirements (Appendix II) that I realised I could get by with much simpler facilities which would take up less space. This permitted the total re-positioning of the MPD and actually made possible the design of a reasonable terminus in the shorter space available by moving the junction. On reflection it seemed to me that this more modest provisioning was more appropriate anyway. The silly thing is that I had come to the same conclusions with 'Marthwaite' and the 'Little Long Drag' systems many years earlier and still fell into the same trap.

I think we have to accept that, unlike real

Plates 119 to 121 These three views show a type of operation which was highly typical of the Settle and Carlisle and, no doubt of other lines too where assisting engines went on the front of the train rather than help push at the rear when long gradients were encountered. They show the detaching of a pilot engine at Ais Gill (Plate 119), the re-start of the train, now single headed (Plate 120) and the pilot engine in the lay-by, waiting its chance to return 'home' (Plate 121). It suggests one possible layout type for the space-starved who must yet have a main line. Why not model the summit of a route and concentrate on all the operational activity associated with getting heavy trains over the hill? Places like Shap Summit and Blackwell were quite a hive of activity and could probably be modelled in less space than a full station.

For the record, the engines are 'Jubilee' No 5594 *Bhopal* and Compound No 1132 (*W. Hubert Foster collection — courtesy NRM*).

119

120

121

railways where the object is to get by with as few locomotives as possible (they are very expensive items both to produce and maintain), the modeller is frequently likely to have too many engines. Some of them can perhaps be found employment in a 'funny train' mode, but what of the others? I think we must try to resist the temptation to have an over-large MPD to house them and make an effort to keep some of them out of sight altogether. Perhaps the best solution is to have a working reserve and keep the surplus stock safely boxed away — or possibly displayed in a showcase and ready for use when required.

Be that as it may, the locomotives themselves should be operated properly, when on the layout. At its most basic this need mean no more than ensuring that vacuum braked stock is operated by a vacuum braked engine. For newer recruits to the hobby, it is perhaps worth recalling that during the loose-coupled freight era, many goods engines had a steam brake only (for their own wheels) and were quite incapable of operating an automatically braked train. However many models we may possess, the most believable operation will be achieved by actually utilising as few of them as possible. In general, this should mean no more than one engine per set of vehicles available, less if possible. Thus, it would be good practice if, on a small terminal type layout, the same locomotive took the train out as brought it in, but the situation may differ between passenger train and freight services.

Taking freight operations first, it was common practice, especially with local and pick-up services, for the train engine to do its own shunting. The luxury of a 'pilot' engine — to perform the miscellaneous odd jobs — was generally confined to larger centres and it is up to the modeller to decide, if he has a large station, whether it needs a station pilot. It would depend on how much work was to be done and whether the train engine(s) needed time for servicing or, if necessary, turning on arrival. Even if the latter was necessary, there may still be sufficient time in the schedule for the local freight engine to both shunt its train (inwards or outwards) and be serviced. Bear in mind that tender-first operation, while disliked, was not ruled out if there was no time to get onto and off the turntable. It was more common on freight services but not unheard of on passenger trains . . . and it was, of course, inevitable in

one direction if the terminus had no turntable. On the whole, therefore, I would think that pilot engines should be kept to the minimum on most layouts and that most of the shunting should be done by the train engines themselves (modellers of Toton marshalling yards or similar can ignore this suggestion!) At Kendal I *have* assumed a pilot, largely because of the probable nature of the operations at certain periods, including trip working of mineral wagons for subsequent despatch and one totally unbalanced passenger service which I cannot roster to another engine. For this reason, the pilot will have to be vacuum fitted. Of course, if the train engines are mostly presumed to have worked a considerable distance when they arrive, there may be a better justification for a station pilot — to allow for the train engines to be serviced.

With passenger trains the problems may be a little different. For a start turn round times may be tighter, barely giving time to run-round, let alone turn or service. In these circumstances, a second engine to take out the incoming train may be a solution; but it would probably look ridiculous if this happened every time. It is better to try and contrive time for a proper turn-round, including servicing if relevant.

I have used the word 'servicing' several times in the last few paragraphs and a word or two on this subject will not be out of place. The servicing of a steam locomotive could cover anything between a quick oil-round by the driver at a station stop to a complete fire drop, coal, turn, water and lighting-up at a more well equipped location. It does not follow that because a depot has coal and water facilities, all engines must use them. Neither need they always use the turntable, if present. In fact, especially where tank engines were widely used, it was quite common for water cranes to be installed on platforms as well as at the depots so that the tank engines (which had no reason to use the turntable) could take water without going on shed — and I am sure that on occasions, tender engines took similar advantage.

As a general rule, the more lengthy servicing (usually preparation for a spell of duty or disposal of the locomotive after such a spell) would be carried out at the engine's home base. Visiting engines might have a quick 'fire clean', or top up their tanks and coal bunkers but they would not normally spend too long on shed. It is therefore quite a good

Plate 122 Certain characteristic operations which were an every day activity defy truly accurate representation in model form and this picture represents one of them. It shows Midland 4–4–0 Class '4' No 993, at Carlisle Durranhill shed, undergoing routine servicing. A convincing scene could be set up for static photography but the best which can be achieved in model operations is simply to allow appropriate time for the supposed activity to take place. This class of engine was particularly associated with the Settle and Carlisle line until withdrawal in 1928 and would be a good choice of prototype for a modeller of this line who wished to establish a sense of 'place' as far as motive power was concerned. Research can often reveal particular types which characterised particular lines or regions (*BR LMR*).

idea to determine, at the outset, which of the locomotive fleet is presumed to be based 'on' the layout and which members are, in effect 'visiting'. In working out schedules, give the 'home' team plenty of time for all their many needs but assume that the 'visitors' are well looked after elsewhere! One could go on at great length on this subject but the intelligent use of common sense and an understanding of the basic principles will be as good a guideline as any other I can give.

One area where, if the modeller is so minded, he can increase his stock in a realistic fashion is in the realm of outgoing trains. Nothing looks more ridiculous on a layout which is being operated to timetable or sequence, whether it be end-to-end or continuous, than to see a locomotive and train, which has supposedly departed for a distant destination, turn up again (sometimes from the wrong direction) a few minutes later. If it is supposed to be on its way to Leeds, then give it time to get there and back before you bring it back in view. The correct working out of the train graph (Appendix I) will soon indicate where this may need attention and possibly even necessitating the quite legitimate provisioning of extra stock. Likewise, any strikingly unusual items of rolling stock (passenger or freight) should not reappear within but a few minutes of being seen to depart . . . although you may get away with it in the case of a humdrum mineral wagon!

Finally, it goes without saying that, in mechanical terms, the locomotive fleet should be as reliable as your own modelling ability can make it. Nothing destroys illusion

123

Plates 123 and 124 The presence of signals can do so much to add authenticity to the scene that is always surprises me that modellers frequently neglect them. The prototype view at Hellifield taken in the late 1950s would look very different without what is, after all, only a simple two-arm gantry in the foreground. However, lurking in the background are a good deal more of these all essential items and it is hard to see how even a modestly complicated layout could look right without them. Even as far back as the first version of 'Marthwaite' Plate 124, I felt that signals were essential and their presence in this picture materially helps to draw attention away from some of the less well modelled aspects of my first 'EM' Gauge attempts (*BR LMR, Jim Russell*).

more quickly than 'finger-prodding' to make engines start or 'jack-rabbit' movements when they are started. Even over-quick train and shunting movements are more acceptable than bad running characteristics.

Signalling

Apart from the trains themselves, signals are one of the few aspects of the model scene which can also be made to operate properly and I feel it is a great pity that so many fine layouts seem to neglect this fact, even to the extent of omitting the signals entirely.

I first appreciated this at 'Marthwaite' where I had a full array of non-working signals which, on reflection, rather spoilt the show by their statuesque immobility! I tried to convince myself that it was because I couldn't make them work; but on the 'Garsdale Road' system I installed working signals and what a difference it made. There were

only four of them (a 'home' and 'starter' in each direction) but, combined with the correct block-bell codes to describe the trains, one could develop quite a sense of anticipation. On balance, I think that the good historical model *must* have working signals, colour light or semaphore, at least for all running lines. Whether this should be extended to ground and shunting signals is, perhaps, more debateable. It may resolve itself to a question of modelling skill or a conscious decision that the ground signals are so small as not to merit making them operational; although they should be modelled if possible.

One of the advantages of signals is that, at least in pre-BR days, they were so visually distinctive between different railways (often between different parts of the same railway) that they play an immense part in creating atmosphere. On my new scheme I want to

124

give the visual impression that the totally non-prototypical continuous link is, in fact, associated with the ex-LNWR Low Gill line — which does not make a physical connection with the ex-Midland portion. I can think of no better way of doing this than by putting an LNWR signalbox and signals at the quite non-existent Lonsdale Junction.

Railway signalling is a fascinating subject but, beyond stating that it should be incorporated, I do not propose to elaborate on the principles here. For one thing, the basic ideas can be gleaned from many standard references and secondly, each railway had its own way of doing things. This can prove a very fruitful research area for the dedicated modeller. However, as part of Appendix III, I thought it helpful to incorporate the correct bell-code signals (LMS) in association with the various train types and locomotive head-codes. Nothing helps so much to convey the correct impression as to use the signalling codes properly.

Conclusion

There are no hard and fast rules to model railway operating. In the last analysis the modeller can do as he pleases and good luck to him. However, I venture to suggest that more permanent satisfaction will be gained by trying to do things properly. We cannot all gain access to the 'rule book' and we may not all be able to draw on personal knowledge — but it is possible to get a bit closer than merely aimless movement of stock. Even the modern railway — simplified though many of its operations are by comparison with former years — can still repay observation. A few hours near or, if one can manage it, inside . an old-fashioned manual signalbox will teach the modeller a great deal, as will a few hours watching, and taking careful note of the shunting activities in a marshalling yard or carriage depot. Much of the action is still recognisably the same as in former years — only the characters on stage have changed.

Appendix 1

Train sequence and timetable planning

Preliminary steps

The basis of any sequence must be a proper evaluation of the real life characteristics of the line to be modelled. In the case of a genuine railway, this means no more than getting hold of a distance and gradient profile of the prototype. For a 'might have been' line, such as my own model, it is helpful to get a copy of the relevant Ordnance Survey map(s) and mark the basic route of the imaginary line. This needs doing with some care and must take account of relief features en route (either by detour, tunnel, viaduct, etc). The economic nature of the supposed route may well determine how much civil engineering can be justified and this must be thought out as the hypothetical line is 'surveyed'.

Stations should be positioned as near to settlements as the lie of the ground will permit. No real railways would make use of unnecessarily tortuous detours or over-steep gradients simply to get a few hundred yards closer to the settlement but, if it was a big enough place, some adjustment may be reasonable. On the other hand, if you are modelling a concept like the Settle–Carlisle, bear in mind that the real railways often made no compromise at all. Kirkby Stephen station (ex-MR) for example, was two miles from the town — any nearer and the MR would have had to steepen the ruling gradient for many miles of main line.

In using Ordnance maps, bear in mind that the most readily available ones (ie, the current editions) include all the built up areas added since the railways were constructed. It is worth doing a bit of 'delving' to discover how big the towns and villages were at the time when the hypothetical line was built and, if necessary, you may find that you can 'route' your line through what is now a modern housing estate to get a better alignment. Having established what seems like a plausible route, it is not difficult to measure distances along the line of the railway to arrive at a total length for the system. Gradients however, are a little more difficult to calculate. The contour lines give a good lead, but it may be necessary to allow for hypothetical embankments or cuttings and it may not be possible to provide for the more subtle gradient changes exhibited by the real railway (eg, 1 in 100, 1 in 110, 1 in 90 following in quick succession). I find, however, that averaging over a mile or two of route is quite satisfactory. As a general guide, it may be helpful to note that a drop of 50 ft height in one mile is a real gradient of 1 in 100 or so (1 in 105.6 to be precise) and that 100 ft per mile is 1 in 50 for practical planning. I mention these values because the Ordnance maps are contoured at 50 feet intervals. The conversion to metric values on many of the more recent maps does not affect this point since it was cheaper to assign metric values to the existing contour lines than to re-survey all the contours at tidy metric intervals!

At the end of all this it is necessary to produce a gradient profile of the line. This is not so that the model can be given correct gradients (unless you so desire), but mainly to enable a realistic calculation of times between stations in the timetable planning stage so as to arrive at a logical sequence. My gradient profile is shown in Fig 24 and the system 'map' in Fig 15.

Establishing the train sequence

There is no doubt in my mind that the best train sequences relate to reality and the basis of all my schedules is the LMS public passenger timetable for the Settle and Carlisle line. My theoretical junction at Dent Head has a real location so one can work out the times at which the real main line trains would have stopped there, had there been a station. This, of course, is possible for any hypothetical line assumed to be in connection with the real life system.

It seemed reasonable to me that most, if not all, the branch services would make connections with the main line stopping trains and on this basis, the framework of the service was established. I also decided that it might be permissible to stop the odd express at Dent Head (to detach a pilot engine perhaps?) and the 'Thames–Forth Express' was chosen for this role (daytime) and the St Pancras–Glasgow sleeping car train (night-time). In the latter case, I also decided that this train would detach/attach through carriages to or from Kendal. This gave ten trains stopping at Dent Head which could be catered for by about half a dozen services on the branch line.

These trains were then timed on the branch by means of the gradient and distance profile, allowing a notional 'one minute per stop' and remembering that Dent Head–Kendal would be quicker than Kendal–Dent Head since most of the line is downhill from Dent Head. When calculating transit times between stations it is difficult to devise hard and fast rules. Generally, trains have speeded up over the years but the best possible advice I can give you is to study those real timetables which quote distances to establish realistic point to point timings — and then add/subtract a small compensating amount for any gradient.

I also decided that Marthwaite and Kendal justified one through service to London in summer and this too was programmed into the system. I have called it 'The Dalesman' and it is assumed to be the Kendal branch equivalent of the 'Lakes Express'. Notionally, the whole train has worked to Skipton where through carriages are detached for Grassington. The train then carries on to Dent Head from whence the main five coach portion goes to Kendal and the balance goes through to Hawes via Garsdale. Prior to arriving at Skipton, it has also picked up a through carriage (at Leeds?) from Bristol to Kendal!

These trains were then put onto a train graph (see below) which enabled me to see

where paths existed for freight and other services. These can be added in the same manner as passenger trains but allowing *at least twice as long* in station to station transit times and also allowing longer at each station for shunting purposes. For most people, this stage will be as far as it is necessary to go and it merely remains to work out the stock requirement to reproduce these patterns. However, if, like me, you have created a rather more complex 'might have been', there is more to do, and it may help those with similar, more complex layout ideas, to explain the additional complications in my own scheme.

In my case I had presumed that Kendal was also in connection with the ex-Furness line from Carnforth to Barrow. I could, therefore, have repeated the Dent Head exercise using Arnside as the junction point; but I did it rather differently. There was, in reality, a service from Arnside to Kendal via Hincaster Junction, Oxenholme (LNWR) and the Windermere line. I took this real service and worked out what the timings would have been if there really had been the alterations of railway geography such as I have envisaged and the real life trains had gone to Kendal Castle (ex-MR) rather than Kendal (ex-LNWR)! This gave a ready made service from Kendal to Arnside and the Barrow line which I knew to be based on reality and which, by sheer fluke, fitted quite well between my fictional services to Dent Head. These were inserted on the graph but only between Natland and Kendal since this was the only bit of the route common to both services (See Fig 15).

There still remained two further problems. I assumed that the model trains leaving Kendal destined for Arnside and/or Barrow arrive at Marthwaite as if they had come from Arnside/Barrow. These, too, needed to be inserted into the programme. This provided additional trains between Marthwaite and Dent Head which, on paper at least, had not originated from Kendal at all. These trains were given fictional departure times to and from Dent Head so that when they finally arrived back at Kendal they represented the real trains from Arnside to Kendal — all very subtle!

Finally, I inserted a railmotor service from Marthwaite to Ingleton via the Low Gill route. This is timed to connect with most services through Marthwaite but in reality will simply leave the bay platform and hide

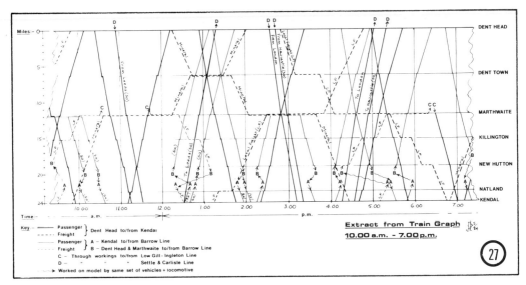

Fig 27 *The train graph* Train graphs can seem very confusing and complex; but if the modeller is prepared to spend a little time in their preparation, they can not only improve the 'believability' of a model but also help develop a real insight into the actual problems of the real railway. To be frank, this graph suggests to me that the number of conflicting contra-directional moves (ie, places at which trains need to pass each other *between* station sites) is barely sufficient to justify the double track throughout which I have assumed. With a little selective re-timing of some trains, one could probably get away with this pattern of traffic on a single track system; but I have assumed the very minimum of trains on the basic graph and I want to be able to insert additional services in the future without disrupting the main theme . . . so I have adopted double lines.

I have also attempted to show the 'change of train identity' by means of a wavy line with arrowhead. It may seem a bit complicated but, in model terms, all that really matters is that the train should not arrive at the second station (in real time terms) before it leaves the first! It does not matter if the difference is only a minute or two because it is not meant to be the same train — if you see what I mean. Thus, there is no need to assume a 'correct to prototype' transit time between, for example, Kendal and Marthwaite, if the engine and train combination is meant to represent a different working on arrival from that which it represented on departure.

Fig 28 This final diagram represents part of what might be called the 'Master Planning Chart' for the operating sequence itself. It gives the basic train arrivals/departures and enables a final check to be made that activities at the two (or more) modelled locations dovetail together in acceptable fashion.

For the operators, an expanded version, *applicable to one location only*, is needed. This should not only give the arrival/departure information but should also include the other activities to be performed — shunting, running round, locomotive servicing etc. As far as possible, to avoid operational chaos, any lengthy sessions of this type of what might be called 'non-timetable' activity should be fitted into the longer gaps between programmed trains. These will always be revealed on the planning chart as areas of 'white paper' provided a constant vertical scale of time is used down the left hand side.

To give a simple example from this chart, there is a long period of 'nil' activity (except for one Saturday only train) at Kendal between '11.15 am' and '12.30 pm'. In my system this amounts to some 14-15 minutes of 'real' time and would be the obvious point at which to service engines or get the next clutch of outgoing freight vehicles ready. In reality, of course, it can still get quite confusing but this approach should give a better chance of success.

itself in a short siding until required to return. This service, too, has its fictional times at places like Kirkby Lonsdale and Ingleton and I was delighted to discover that they made quite reasonable connections with real LMS trains on this route. It was only at

this point in my case, that I could finally insert freight services into the system. Most freights are in the nature of pick-up services and, as with passenger trains, the Kendal–Arnside pick-ups change identity en route. Just to add a bit of confusion, these trains,

KENDAL BRANCH – OPERATING SEQUENCE   (28)

PASSENGER SETS:-	CODE	LOCOMOTIVE DUTIES	
Kendal/Dent Head A	A	Local Passenger	1
Kendal/Dent Head B	B *	"	2 *
Kendal District No.1.	1	"	3
Kendal District No.2.	2 *	"	4 *
Steam Railmotor	R *	Motor Fitted Loco	5 *
"Dalesman" Express	D	Express Loco	6
Leeds Express	L	" (SO)	7
Newcastle Express	N	Kendal Pilot Loco	8 *
Sleeping Cars	S	Local Freight	9 *
		"	10
* Located at Kendal at start of		"	11 *
operational sequence		Heavy Mineral	12

'REAL' TIME	'BOOK' TIME	KENDAL CASTLE — OPERATION	LOCO	STOCK	MARTHWAITE — OPERATION	LOCO	STOCK
1 00							
	9 25				Local Passenger Dent Head - Kendal	2	B
	9 30	Local Freight Departs for Arnside	11	Goods	Local Passenger Kendal - Dent Head	1	A
	9 35				Railmotor departs for Ingleton	5	R
	9 50	Minerals depart for Dent Head	12	Min	Local passenger departs for Barrow (SO)	3	1
	9 55	Local Passenger arrives ex-Dent Head	2	B			
	10 00				Local Freight arrives ex-Arnside	11	Goods
	10 05				Local passenger departs for Arnside (SX)	3	1
1 10	10 09	(SO) Local Passenger arrives ex-Arnside	3	1			
	10 30				Local Freight departs for Ingleton Line	11	Goods
	10 37	(SX) Local Passenger arrives ex-Grange O.S.	3	1	Minerals arrive ex-kendal	12	Min
	10 40				Railmotor arrives ex-Ingleton	5	R
	10 45				Local Passenger Dent Head - Kendal		A
	10 46				Railmotor departs for Ingleton	5	R
1 20							
	11 10	Local Passenger Departs for Dent Head	2	B	Express (SO) Leeds - Kendal	7	L
	11 15	Local Passenger arrives ex-Dent Head	1	A			
	11 32	(SO) Express arrives ex-Leeds/Bradford &c	7	L			
	11 40				Local Passenger Kendal - Dent Head	2	B
	11 45				Local Freight arrives ex-Ingleton Line	11	Goods
1 30	11 50				Railmotor arrives ex-Ingleton	5	R
	12 15				Minerals depart for Dent Head	12	Min
	12 25				Local freight departs for Arnside	11	Goods
	12 30	Local Freight arrives ex-Arnside	11	Goods	Local passenger Arnside - Dent Head (SX)	3	1
	12 32	(SX) Local Passenger departs for Barrow	3	1	Railmotor departs for Ingleton (SX)	5	R
	12 32	(SO) Express departs for Leeds &c.	7	L			
1 40	12 40	(SO) Local Passenger departs for Barrow	3	1	Express arrives ex-Kendal } (SO)	7	L
	12 54				Express departs for Leeds &c } (SO)		
	1 10	Local Freight departs for Dent Head	10	Goods	Local passenger Barrow - Dent Head (SO)	3	1
	1 15				Local passenger Dent Head - Kendal	2	B
	1 17				Railmotor departs for Ingleton (SO)	5	R
1 50	1 35				Local passenger Dent Head - Sedgewick	4	2
	1 45	Local Passenger arrives ex-Dent Head	2	B			
	1 56	Local Passenger arrives ex-Barrow (SO)	4	2			
	2 06	Local Passenger arrives ex-Barrow (SX)	4	2	Empty minerals arrive ex-Dent Head	12	Min
	2 15	Local Passenger departs for Grange O.S	4	2	Local freight arrives ex-kendal	10	Goods
2 00	2 20	Local Passenger departs for Dent Head	1	A	Railmotor arrives ex-Ingleton	5	R
					Local passenger arrives ex-Sedgewick	4	2
	2 50				"Dalesman" arrives ex-St Pancras	6	D
					Local Passenger Kendal-Dent Head	1	A
					"Dalesman" departs for Kendal	6	D
	3 00				Express arrives ex-Newcastle	7	N
					Railmotor departs for Ingleton	5	R
	3 05				Express departs for Kendal	7	N
2 10	3 10	"The Dalesman" (ex-St Pancras) arrives	6	D			
	3 20	(SO) Express arrives ex-Newcastle	7	N	Local passenger departs for Sedgewick	4	2
	3 36	Local Passenger arrives ex-Grange O.S.	4	2			
	3 40				Empty minerals depart for Kendal	12	Min
	3 51				Local freight departs for Dent Head	10	Goods

having left Kendal, terminate at Marthwaite, then divert down the Ingleton line (in theory as far as Kirkby Lonsdale) to collect mineral wagons, etc.

Mineral services were programmed separately both to add to the number of freight workings and because of the more than normal quarry traffic envisaged. The intention throughout is that the services planned should have a reasonably logical background and yet allow for considerable variation in train loads depending upon circumstances. In practice, it is probably best to work out all these requirements in parallel with the production of a train graph. My advice is to do the latter in rough form first (and in pencil!) and only when this is resolved, make a fair copy.

The train graph

On the basis that following prototype practice is always a sound notion, I have always developed my model sequences to the extent of producing a train graph in real time terms. I did it for 'Marthwaite', 'Garsdale Road' and the 'Little Long Drag' and I am using my current scheme to demonstrate the method here.

The first requirement is a large sheet of graph paper to take a full day (in hours/ minutes) along the horizontal axis. It need not span 24 hours unless your services so demand. In my case it runs from about 4:30 am to 12:30 am (ie, 20 hours). I like to use about 1 in–2 in for each hour along the horizontal axis. The vertical axis represents the distance(s) between stations. Any suitable scale will do but stations must be at the correct scale distance apart and I find it helpful to have the vertical axis repeated on both left and right hand sides of the sheet.

The trains are then plotted. Start at the departure time opposite the station in question, mark it on the graph, then mark the arrival time at the next station and join the two together. The line runs horizontally to represent the period of each stop and then the process is repeated. The slope of the line reflects the speed, the steeper the slope, the greater the speed. It is actually simpler to do than to describe and I find it easier to plot all the trains in one direction first. Trains in the

opposite direction will, obviously, slope the opposite way and these can then be added.

Start with the scheduled passenger trains and this will then reveal where a sufficient interval exists for a slower moving freight train. The graph will show where, say, a passenger service can overtake a goods train (shunting?) and where trains travelling in opposite directions will pass each other. On this latter point, the graph will also indicate whether or not it is reasonable to presume double or single track on the 'main' line. If there are few conflicting movements in opposite directions, it might well be worthwhile to examine the sequence to see whether, by selective re-timing, trains travelling in opposite directions can pass each other at stations rather than out in the country. No real railway would provide a double track if the traffic on offer could be handled by a single line with passing places and the train graph will reveal whether or not this is a realistic proposition.

In practical terms I have found it helpful to mark passenger and freight trains in a differentiated way on the train graph — eg, solid lines and broken lines although different colours could be equally effective. In Fig 27 I have shown only a portion of the complete sequence.

Having established a comprehensive train graph, the final phase is to translate the information into a series of working instructions (for each modelled location) for the operational side of the layout. In Fig 28, I have appended the working instructions for Marthwaite and Kendal based on part of the working timetable represented by the portion of the train graph at Fig 27. Careful comparison of the two should serve to explain how the whole system functions.

The working instructions can be written either as a complete sequence of activities (as illustrated) or can be turned into a series of individual cards, taken consecutively and each bearing a single instruction for the benefit of the layout operators. The working instructions should specify both the nature of the operation to be undertaken and the stock/locomotive(s) concerned. In fact, it is only at this point that the real stock requirement of the layout can be fully analysed.

Appendix II

Rational stock planning

In stock planning the principal objective is to work out the minimum requirement of loco-motives and stock on the basis that the real railway normally would not, and generally did not provide more equipment than was needed to perform the tasks. In model terms this involves using the train graph to estab-lish the smallest quota of locomotives and rolling stock which will enable the modeller to reproduce this characteristic in a believ-able way. It should be stated from the outset that this quota will not necessarily equate with the smallest number of models needed actually to operate the layout. In extremis one could probably use one set of carriages for all passenger trains and one engine/brake for all freight trains — but realism would be sacrificed. The aim is to produce a proper balance and for this, it is necessary to refer again to the train graph.

Planning the right number of trains

In order to determine the correct number of trains (and in this context I also include the locomotive) it is only necessary to find out the fewest number which would be needed *in reality* to operate the services. Thus, if one set of carriages could actually shuttle to and fro along the line and cope with all the booked workings, then the real railway would only use one set. There may be the odd extra carriage at busy times but one basic set would suffice.

However, it is likely that even a modestly busy line would need more than one set. In my own case, for example, the train graph revealed that the 7:30 am from Kendal to Dent Head could come back as the 9:00 am Dent Head to Kendal, arriving at 9:55 am. Therefore, a second set of vehicles (including engine) would be needed at Kendal for the

9:02 am to Dent Head. Working through the whole sequence in this way and assuming that each set would come back at the next available booked time, as far as possible, I discovered that two sets of coaches on *each route* would in fact suffice and that they would all end the working day in the same location as they had started it. This is always a desirable situation to aim for, otherwise one may have to add non-revenue earning empty stock movements to re-establish the balance. The real railways did this — but not unless they had to!

A similar principle should be applied to freight workings. In this case, it is the engine and brake van which need to be balanced, it being assumed that the load carrying wagons are 'in transit' to and from more distant destinations. In practice, of course, except in the case of unusual and easily identifiable vehicles, one can permit a degree of 'to-ing and fro-ing' of the more common types — open wagons, box vans, etc. This exercise will not only help establish the number of model trains required but will also reveal where, on the layout, the stock will start and finish the daily round. This, in turn, will give some indication of the size and nature of the facilities needed both at the modelled sta-tions and in the off-stage storage area(s). As a corollary, it will also reveal those periods in the operational sequence when either one particular station, or the storage roads them-selves, may become a little overcrowded. It is better to find out at this stage than devote hours to making the model and find out the hard way that an extra siding should have been planned or, even more annoying, that too much trackage has been laid at a high cost in both time and money. It was by perform-ing this exercise in detail that I discovered I could manage with a fairly modest MPD at Kendal and thus design the terminus into the (preferred) smaller amount of space.

So, having worked out the number of trains, and where they and their locomotives will normally be based at the start of the day, it only remains to work out, more precisely, the appropriate types and quantities of locomotives and stock. For the most part this should readily be possible by following the principles discussed in Chapter 7. One area may, however, give difficulty — the rational planning of freight vehicle provisioning.

Freight traffic and rolling stock planning

The usual trouble for most people in this area is a lack of detailed knowledge of the prototype — especially as some of the historical periods most favoured by modellers recede further and further into the past. I am no exception to the norm, but many years ago, when researching the Settle–Carlisle line, I was lucky enough to examine comprehensive traffic details at all stations for the 1876–1923 and 1947–63 periods. This gave me a very useful insight into the problem and I tend to use this knowledge, almost without realising it, when working out trains. In essence, the problem breaks down into two areas, the type of traffic to be handled and, secondly, the quantity.

As far as type is concerned, the modeller must make his own choice, depending on the 'geography' of his system, real or imagined. Within limits and depending on historical period chosen, the railways have, in their time, handled just about every form of traffic from circus animals to aeroplanes! Provided the traffic type makes economic sense there is no good reason why the modeller cannot be as exotic as he likes, provided it is not overdone and that the 'bread and butter' traffic (coal, general merchandise, etc) is catered for. Thus, in my own case, I felt that I could justifiably incorporate heavy extra mineral traffic, a limited amount of specialised timber traffic — for a hypothetical paper works, and a little more livestock traffic than usual. This would then add some variety to the otherwise very orthodox traffic envisaged.

The matter of quantity is more difficult to generalise. In the case of general purpose traffic the amount is closely related to the size (in population terms) of the community being served. Thus one has to have some conception of the type of settlement being

represented. In my case, I assumed that Marthwaite and Kendal would be somewhat similar in their needs to Settle or Appleby — or near enough to take the two latter places as a guide, tending to assume that there would be slightly more traffic at Kendal than at Marthwaite. I have also tried to bear in mind that both locations in reality had another station (ex-LNWR) and this would probably influence traffic volume on the 'new' Midland line, especially at the Kendal end where the (existing) LNWR freight yard was quite large.

On this basis, I came to the following approximate conclusions for each of the two principal stations:

Cattle: some 1,000–1,500 wagon loads per year.
Coal: some 6,000 tons per year.
Loco coal (Kendal): 4,000–6,000 tons per year.
Milk: two or three vans per day.
General freight: some 5,000–10,000 tons annually.
Timber: three or four wagon loads per week.

In addition, I calculated that the quarries on the line would generate an output somewhat similar to that of the Horton-in-Ribblesdale or Ribblehead areas and I put in a notional 100,000–150,000 tons per year for the branch as a whole.

Turning these figures into daily wagon needs was not too difficult on the basis of normal average loads, say 8 tons for mineral and 2–3 tons for general freight. It is essentially a question of arithmetic and I gave the following daily approximations for each location:

Cattle Wagons: 4–6 wagons per day (could be operated once or twice weekly as a cattle special in due course).
General Coal: 3–4 wagons per day.
Loco coal (Kendal): 1–2 wagons per day (NB: loco coal wagons were often of larger capacity than domestic coal).
Milk: 2–3 vans per day.
General freight: 10–12 vehicles per day.
Timber (Kendal): Averaging perhaps 1 vehicle per day but probably consigned once or twice per week as a 'block' load.
Minerals: 40–50 wagons per day (at least), mostly from Marthwaite (likely to be two special workings).

Obviously not all the wagons would be on

the layout at any one time. Some would be in the storage area, ie, in transit to or from the system. Moreover, one has also to allow for wagons lying idle. Nevertheless, from these figures and the train graph, it is possible to work out without too much trouble, the total wagon fleet to be modelled.

It is my experience that for the 'anonymous' wagons — of which it may be safely presumed there were numerous identical examples in use (save for their running numbers), it is not necessary to stock the layout with the full quota needed. I have found that *for each type* about 50 per cent above the likely number of such vehicles to be found on any one train is about right. To give a simple example I will take the mineral traffic on my own system, where the thought of making 50 or more mineral wagons was not greeted with any great enthusiasm! I argued that, given the gradients I have postulated (Fig 24), a 50 wagon train would be out of the question and that two 20–25 wagon trains would be more likely. These trains could then, in addition, carry the occasional timber and loco coal vehicles which the sequence demanded. It is, by the way, perfectly legitimate to have non-mineral vehicles on a mineral train!

I have worked out that by using the same wagons again, I can manage with about 75 per cent of the 'daily' requirement. It is still a large number but does show some reduction. Essentially, about one third will be at the quarry site (loaded) and when the empties arrive, half the empties will be loaded for return (while the train goes to Kendal and back) and the other half left behind. This will then give two thirds 'loaded' — the basis of the outgoing loaded train, leaving the residual empties to be loaded before the next working. I must confess that having seen the various quarry operations on the Settle–Carlisle line does help here and, at the time of writing, there are still too few mineral wagons on my latest layout — but this is only a matter of time to resolve.

As far as general merchandise vehicles are concerned, a loaded van looks the same as an unloaded one and a sheeted down open wagon bringing in one kind of cargo, will not look very different when it departs with a supposedly different cargo — so it is quite feasible to allow some doubling up in this area. Genuinely open vehicles (ie, not sheeted over) are best fitted with detachable 'loads' to simulate different traffic flows but the individual modeller will speedily be able to resolve these issues for himself. It is worth doing, however, because it adds purpose to the operation and hence realism to the scene.

At this point it would be tempting to digress at greater detail into the issues raised briefly in Chapter 7 concerning the actual operation of a model railway system; but this is less a function of the historical approach than that of model railway operation generally. I shall, therefore, resist this temptation and confine my final supplementary remarks to a brief résumé of some of the historical aspects of LMS train operation as revealed by the official company records. For convenience, I have separated them out as Appendix III.

Appendix III

Selected Extracts from the LMS general appendix to the Working Timetable of 1937

The following facsimile pages from the LMS general appendix are selected from the full 95 page set of instructions covering every conceivable aspect of train operation and safety. They are probably the pages of most relevance to modellers.

EXTRACT FROM THE REGULATION OF RAILWAYS ACT, 1889.

INSTRUCTIONS WITH RESPECT TO CONTINUOUS BRAKES.

A.—PASSENGER TRAINS.

1.—All passenger trains must be worked with the continuous brake in use by the Company.

To facilitate working, however, the following exceptional arrangements are allowed :-

In passenger trains a proportion of unbraked vehicles may be run on the following conditions :—

(a) That all such vehicles shall have continuous pipes of the pattern in use upon the trains with which they are running.

(b) That the proportion of such vehicles shall not exceed one in four in every passenger train running a distance not exceeding 19 miles without a stop.

(c) That the proportion of such vehicles shall not exceed one in six in every passenger train running a distance exceeding 10 miles without a stop.

Provided that for the purpose of conditions (b) and (c) the number of vehicles forming a train be counted as follows:—

Tender engine, 6 or 8 coupled	as 4 vehicles
Tender engine, 4 coupled	as 3 „
Tank engine, 4 or 6 wheeled coupled	as 2 „
Coaching vehicles, 8 or 12 wheeled	as 2 „
Coaching vehicles, 4 or 6 wheeled	as 1 vehicle.
Horse box, carriage truck, fish van or other 4-wheeled vehicle not carrying passengers	as ½ „

Table showing what proportion of unbraked vehicles (which must be fitted with continuous pipes) may be attached to a passenger train RUNNING **NOT MORE THAN 10 MILES** WITHOUT A STOP.			Table showing what proportion of unbraked vehicles (which must be fitted with continuous pipes) may be attached to a passenger train RUNNING **MORE THAN 10 MILES** WITHOUT A STOP.		
To a train (including engine) consisting of braked vehicles equal to—		Unbraked vehicles equal to—	To a train (including engine) consisting of braked vehicles equal to—		Unbraked vehicles equal to—
3	may be added	1	3	may be added	½
3½	„ „	1	3½	„ „	½
4	„ „	1	4	„ „	½
4½	„ „	1½	4½	„ „	½
5	„ „	1½	5	„ „	1
5½	„ „	1½	5½	„ „	1

6	,,	,,	2		6	,,	,,	1
6½	,,	,,	2		6½	,,	,,	1
7	,,	,,	2		7	,,	,,	1
7½	,,	,,	2½		7½	,,	,,	1½
8	,,	,,	2½		8	,,	,,	1½
8½	,,	,,	2½		8½	,,	,,	1½
9	,,	,,	3		9	,,	,,	1½
9½	,,	,,	3		9½	,,	,,	1½
10	,,	,,	3		10	,,	,,	2
10½	,,	,,	3½		10½	,,	,,	2
11	,,	,,	3½		11	,,	,,	2
11½	,,	,,	3½		11½	,,	,,	2
12	,,	,,	4		12	,,	,,	2
12½	,,	,,	4		12½	,,	,,	2½
13	,,	,,	4		13	,,	,,	2½
13½	,,	,,	4½		13½	,,	,,	2½
14	,,	,,	4½		14	,,	,,	2½
14½	,,	,,	4½		14½	,,	,,	2½
15	,,	,,	5		15	,,	,,	3

2.—Except as hereinafter provided the last vehicle of every passenger train must be fitted with the continuous brake of the pattern in use upon the train.

Where necessary to avoid delay in working, one vehicle only, not being a passenger carrying vehicle, may be placed in the rear of any such train without being fitted with the continuous brake or with the continuous pipe, except on those sections of the line where the vehicles behind the rear brake van must be provided with the continuous brake or where the practice of running vehicles behind the rear brake van is prohibited. (*See respective Sectional Appendices for sections of line affected.*)

NOTE.—Grooms or attendants travelling in horse boxes, etc., are not counted as passengers.

B.—MIXED TRAINS.

1.—" Mixed " trains for the conveyance of freight and passengers, in which the freight wagons are not required to have continuous brakes, may be run, subject to the following conditions, namely:—

(a) That the engine, tender and passenger vehicles of such " mixed " trains shall be provided with continuous brakes worked from the engine.

(b) That the freight wagons shall be conveyed behind the passenger vehicles with brake van, or brake vans, in the proportion of one brake van with a tare of 10 tons for every 10 wagons, or one brake van with a tare of 13 or more tons for every 15 wagons, or one brake van with a tare of 16 or more tons for every 20 wagons, or fractional parts of 10, 15 or 20 wagons respectively.

(c) That the total number of vehicles of all descriptions of any such " mixed " train shall not exceed 30, except in the case of a circus train when the number shall not exceed 35.

(d) That all such trains shall stop at stations, so as to avoid a longer run than 10 miles without stopping, but nothing in these regulations shall require a stop to be made between two stations should the distance between them exceed 10 miles.

The distance over which a circus train may run without a stop may be increased to a maximum of 50 miles.

2.—Upon lines where the maximum speed of trains is limited to 25 miles per hour, all trains may be " mixed."

Upon lines where no trains are booked to travel between stations at an average speed of more than 35 miles per hour, half of the total number of passenger trains may be " mixed." Authority to work a larger proportion of " mixed " trains must be obtained from the Minister of Transport.

Upon lines where trains are booked to travel between stations at an average speed exceeding 35 miles per hour, the like authority must be obtained before any " mixed " trains are run.

Circus trains may be run without such authority during the period from March 31st to November 30th in any year whether the maximum average speed of trains run on the section of line concerned is limited or not.

In no case must the speed of a circus train exceed 30 miles per hour.

3.—Trains for the conveyance of horses, cattle or other stock, when vehicles are added for the conveyance of passengers, shall be subject to the same regulations and conditions as apply to "mixed" trains, but drovers, grooms or other persons travelling in charge of such stock shall not be deemed to be passengers

A passenger vehicle provided for the special accommodation of persons travelling in charge of stock must, however, be marshalled next the engine, and be provided with the continuous brake worked from the engine.

4.—When, in addition to one goods brake van at the rear of a "mixed" train, a passenger brake vehicle is included as part of the continuously braked stock, it will not be necessary for a guard to ride in the passenger brake vehicle. If the composition of the train necessitates a second (or third) goods brake van, a second (or third) guard will be necessary, unless communication between the vans is such as to enable one guard to operate efficiently the hand brakes on the vans.

All trains booked to be run as "mixed" will be so shown in the Working Time Tables, and the foregoing regulations will apply to such trains.

The expression circus train means a "mixed" train in which livestock, traction engines, trailers, caravans, tenting and other equipment and circus employees belonging to a touring circus are exclusively being conveyed.

NOTE.—The above regulations do not apply to troop trains.

TROOP TRAINS.

Troop trains timed at speeds not exceeding THIRTY-FIVE MILES PER HOUR may be made up to a maximum of 30 vehicles over sections of the line where there is no specially restricted load on account of severe gradients, provided the whole of the vehicles are fitted with the continuous brake or through pipe, connected up and working throughout the train. Each vehicle, bogie or otherwise to count as one. Total tonnage not to exceed that laid down for the lines concerned.

WORKING OF CIRCUS TRAINS.

When it is desired to run a circus train 50 miles without stopping and such train starts from a point at which no C. & W. staff is employed, the train must be stopped at the first point at which such staff is available to enable the necessary examination to be carried out.

SHUNTING OF PASSENGER TRAINS FOR OTHER TRAINS TO PASS.

Referring to Rule 146, clause (c); passenger trains must not be shunted from an up to a down running line, or vice versa, for another train to pass.

This instruction does not prohibit a passenger train being shunted on to a branch line at a junction or into a bay line at a station.

ENGINE HEAD LAMPS.

All L.M.S. engines, whether working over the L.M.S. or other Companies' lines, and the engines of other Companies working over the L.M.S. lines, must, unless instructions are issued to the contrary, carry white head lights arranged as under, and trains must be signalled by the bell signals shown :—

Description of train.	Bell Signal.	Head light.
1.—Express passenger train, or break-down van train going to clear the line, or light engine going to assist disabled train, or fire brigade train	4	
2.—Ordinary passenger train, or break-down van train not going to clear the line ... ... Branch passenger train (where authorised) ... ... Rail motor or motor train with engine leading ... (When running with driving compartment leading rail motors or motor trains will carry the headlamp on the same bracket as used for the tail lamp.) NOTE.—*For arrangements in regard to electric trains see the various electric line instruction books.*	3—1 1—3 3—1—2	

3.—Parcels, newspaper, fish, meat, fruit, milk, horse, or perishable train, composed of coaching stock	1—1—3	
4.—Empty coaching stock train	2—2—1	
Fitted freight, fish or cattle train with the continuous brake in use on NOT LESS than one-third the vehicles	5	
5.—Express freight or cattle train with the continuous brake on less than one-third the vehicles, but in use on four vehicles connected to the engine indicated by ✚ in the Working Time Tables	2—2—3	
Express freight or cattle train not fitted with the continuous brake, or with the continuous brake in use on LESS than four vehicles	3—2	
6.—Through freight train, or ballast train conveying workmen and running not less than 15 miles without stopping	1—4	
7.—Light engine, or light engines coupled together	2—3	
Engine with one or two brakes	1—3—1	
8.—Through mineral or empty wagon train	4—1	
9.—Freight train stopping at intermediate stations, or ballast train running short distance	3	
Branch freight train (where authorised)	1—2	
Ballast train, freight train, or officers' special requiring to stop in section or at intermediate siding in section.	1—2—2	
10.—Shunting engines working exclusively in station yards and sidings.	Must, whilst in those sidings, carry one red head light and one red tail light.	

The lamps must be carried in position day and night.

Note.—*Local exceptional arrangements are shown in the respective Sectional Appendices.*
When a train running on the L.M.S. Railway is worked by two engines attached in front of the train, the second engine must not carry head lamps.

SIGNALLING OF TRAINS CONVEYING SPECIAL HORSE OR PIGEON TRAFFIC.

Where instructions are given in the Special Train Notices for trains conveying special horse or pigeon traffic and composed of coaching stock to be signalled by the bell signal of 5 beats (given 3 pause 1 pause 1), such trains must carry No. 3 headlights and take precedence of all other trains except express passenger trains, breakdown van trains going to clear the line, light engines going to assist disabled trains, or fire brigade trains.

TAIL LAMPS AND SIDE LIGHTS ON TRAINS.

Referring to Rule 120; the following instructions apply to trains working over the L.M.S. Railway :—

Mixed trains with a freight train guard's brake van in rear must carry side lamps as laid down for freight trains.

Except where instructions are issued to the contrary, all freight trains or engines with freight train guard's brake van or vans must carry side lights on the rear brake van as follows :—

(A) On main lines where there are only two lines and on single lines......... One red tail light and two red side lights.

(B) On main lines where there are three or four running lines :—

   (i.) On the fast line............... One red tail light and two red side lights.

   (ii.) On the slow, goods, or loop lines................................. One red side light on the side of the van furthest away from the fast line, one white side light on the side of the van nearest the fast line, and one red tail light (*see Note*).

(C) On goods or loop lines adjoining four main lines............................. One red tail light only. Side lamps must be removed when the train has passed into the loop.

Note.—Certain brake vans are provided with side lamps which cannot be turned, or which, when turned to show a white light to the rear, show a red light to the front. In these cases the instructions in paragraph (B) (ii.) will not apply, and the side lamp instead of being turned must be removed. A signalman will not be required to send the " Tail or side light out, or improper side light exhibited " signal when a train passes his box with side light removed as directed.

Where side lights are shown to be carried the side lamps must, except in the case of local trips, be carried on the rear brake van during daylight as well as during darkness.

The instructions in clause (a) of Rule 120 respecting the carrying, cleaning, trimming, and lighting of tail lamps also apply to light engines.

Tail lamps on passenger trains.—The guard, or rear guard where there is more than one, must see that the tail lamp is properly fixed before signalling the train away. This will not, however, relieve from responsibility any of the platform staff who should affix tail lamps.

Station Masters and inspectors must pay special attention when vehicles are attached or detached, and see that the tail lamp is in its proper position.

A clean trimmed tail lamp must be carried inside the rear van of all trains provided with gas tail lamps, and in each portion where there is more than one van provided with gas tail lamps.

L.N.E. Railway (G.E. Section) coaching stock brake vans with fitted tail lamps.—When one of these brake vans is the rear vehicle on a train, the fixed tail lamp must not be used and an ordinary oil tail lamp must be carried both by day and by night.

Extinguishing lights in side and tail lamps.—At the completion of the train journey and after the train is shunted into a siding clear of the running lines, the guard, before leaving the train, must, unless instructions are issued to the contrary, extinguish the lights in the side and tail lamps.

Freight, etc., trains, assisted in rear—Tail and side lamps.

Referring to Rule 133; when a freight train is assisted in rear by an engine or by an engine propelling one or two brake vans, the guard of the freight train must remove his tail lamp. When the train is assisted by an engine drawing one or two brake vans, the guard of the freight train must, in addition to removing the tail lamp, remove his side lamps, and side lamps must be carried on the rearmost brake van attached to the assisting engine.

Appendix IV

'Sidestrip' diagram of the Settle and Carlisle line

This type of diagram was used by the time-table planners whenever they needed to know the line capacity in terms of siding lengths or yard capacity. Thus, the lengths of lay-bys (LB) are marked according to the number of standard four-wheel wagons which could be accommodated, including train engine. Yard capacity is also quoted in terms of four-wheel wagons. A 'standard' wagon was, in effect, the standard railway clearing house mineral wagon and adjustments were made for longer/shorter vehicles.

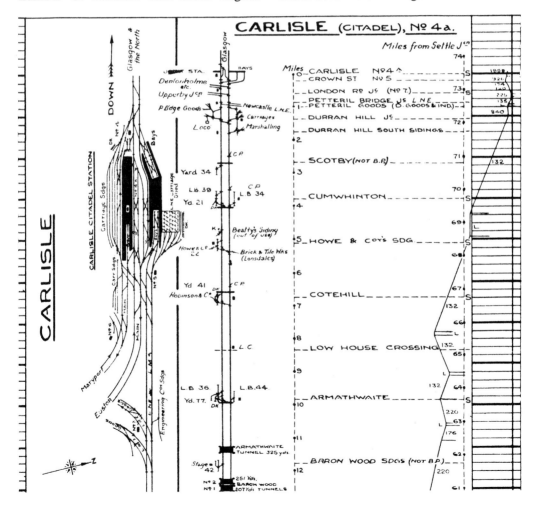

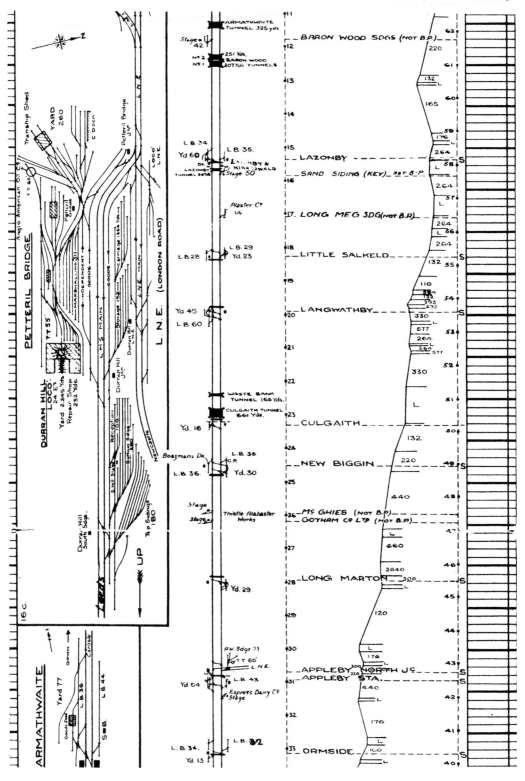

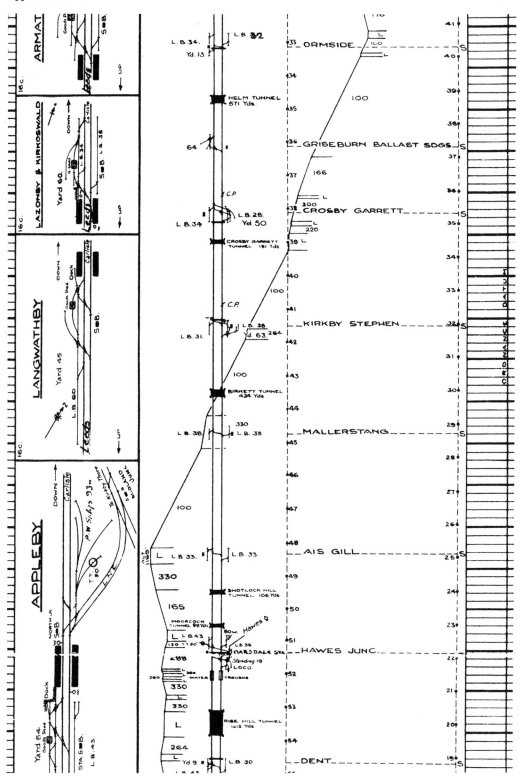

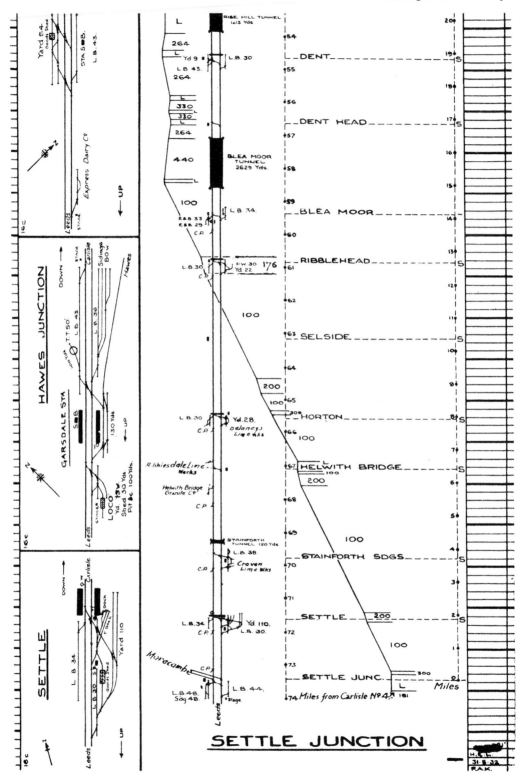

SETTLE JUNCTION

Index